CAR

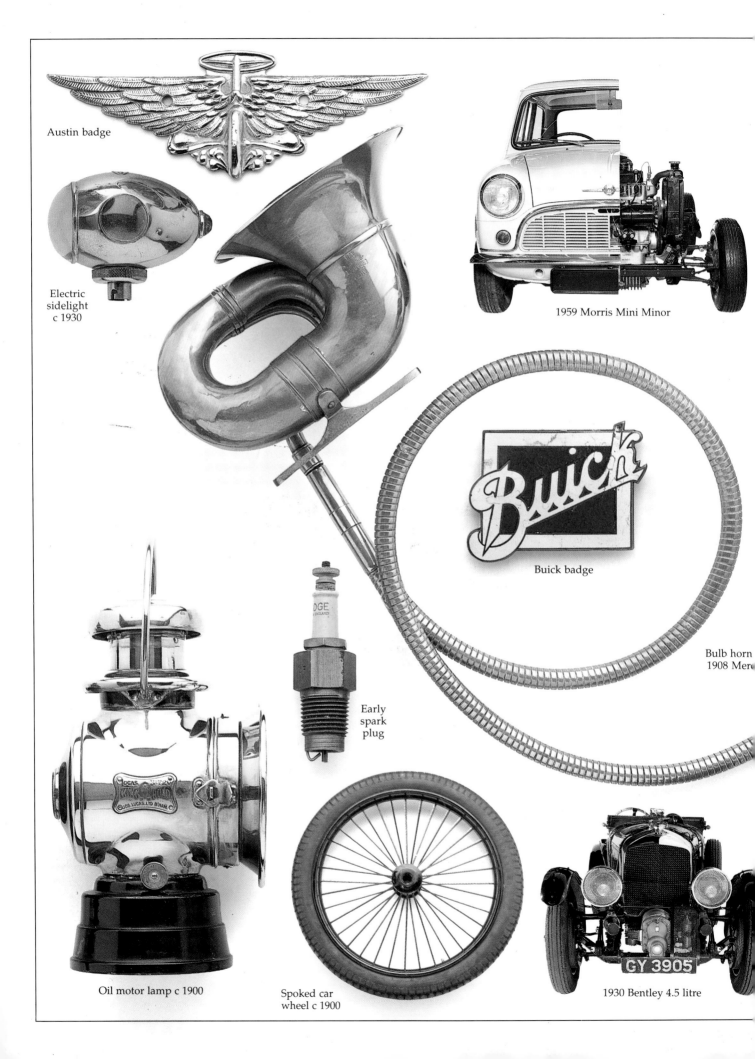

Austin badge

Electric
sidelight
c 1930

1959 Morris Mini Minor

Buick badge

Bulb horn
1908 Mer(

Oil motor lamp c 1900

Early
spark
plug

Spoked car
wheel c 1900

1930 Bentley 4.5 litre

Headlight bulbs c 1900

EYEWITNESS  GUIDES

Ferrari

Ferrari badge

CAR

Written by
RICHARD SUTTON

ANNAN ACADEMY
LIBRARY

1930 Bentley
4.5 litre

Early spark plug

1935 Auburn 851 Speedster

DK

DORLING KINDERSLEY • LONDON

Fuel injector

A DORLING KINDERSLEY BOOK

Project editor John Farndon
Design Mathewson Bull
Managing editor Sophie Mitchell
Senior art editor Julia Harris
Editorial director Sue Unstead
Art director Anne-Marie Bulat
Special photography Dave King
and Mike Dunning

Steering rack

This Eyewitness ® Guide has been
conceived by Dorling Kindersley Limited
and Editions Gallimard

First published in Great Britain in 1990
by Dorling Kindersley Limited,
9 Henrietta Street, London, WC2E 8PS

Reprinted 1990, 1992, 1993, 1994, 1996

British Library Cataloguing in Publication Data
Sutton, Richard
Car.
1. Cars
I. Title II. Series
629.2'222

ISBN 0-86318-412-X

Color reproduction by Colourscan, Singapore
Typeset by Windsorgraphics, Ringwood, Hampshire
Printed in Singapore by Toppan Printing Co. (S) Pte Ltd.

Telescopic damper
and coil spring

Early spark plugs

Contents

Early spark plugs

Horseless power

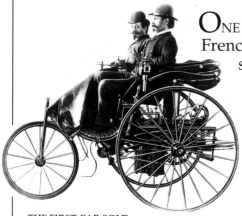

THE FIRST CAR SOLD
Dating from 1888, this is an advert for the first car ever sold, Karl Benz's three-wheeler "Patent-Motorwagen".

ONE AFTERNOON in the summer of 1862, a Frenchman called Étienne Lenoir gingerly started the engine he had built and mounted between the wheels of an old horse cart. Minutes later, the little cart was trundling through the Vincennes forest near Paris, moved only by the slowly thumping engine. It was a historic moment, for Lenoir's self-propelled cart was launched into a world of horse-drawn carriages and stage-coaches, cart-tracks and dust roads – a world that would soon vanish forever. Lenoir was not the first to build a "horseless carriage"; carriages powered by cumbersome steam engines had already been made for almost a century. His breakthrough was the invention of the compact "internal combustion" engine (pp. 42-45), which worked by burning gas inside a cylinder. A few years later, gas engines were made to run on petrol and soon the first experimental motor cars were being built. In 1885, the first car to be sold to the public rolled out of the workshops of Karl Benz in Mannheim in Germany. The age of the automobile had begun.

MAKING A DASH FOR IT
The front panel of many early cars was reminiscent of the "dashboard" of the horse carriage – so-called because it stopped the coachman being "dashed" by flying stones thrown up by the horses. Even today, a car's instrument panel may still be referred to as the dash.

COACH-WORK
The first motor cars owed a great deal to the horse carriage. Indeed, many pioneering cars were simply horse carts with an engine – which is one reason they were known as "horseless carriages". Even purpose-built cars were usually made by a traditional coachbuilder, using centuries-old skills and techniques.

TAKE AWAY THE HORSE . . .
The similarities between horse carriages and the first cars are obvious. Note the large wheels, boat-shaped body, high driver's seat and dashboard.

COACH SPRING
Early cars had curved iron springs to soften the ride – just like those used on horse coaches throughout the 19th century.

Coach spring

Engine

HILL-CLIMBING
Many early cars could not climb hills because they had no gears; they simply came to a standstill and then rolled backwards. But on the Benz Victoria of 1890, the driver was given a lever to slip the leather drive belt on to a small pulley. This meant the wheels turned slower, but the extra leverage enabled the car to climb uphill. The chain-driven Velo had three of these forward gear pulleys and one reverse.

HORSE SENSE
The first cars were notoriously unreliable. This cartoon suggested it might be just as well to take a couple of horses along in case of breakdowns.

Massive flywheel to keep the engine running smoothly

Rear wheels driven by chains looped round big cogs on either wheel

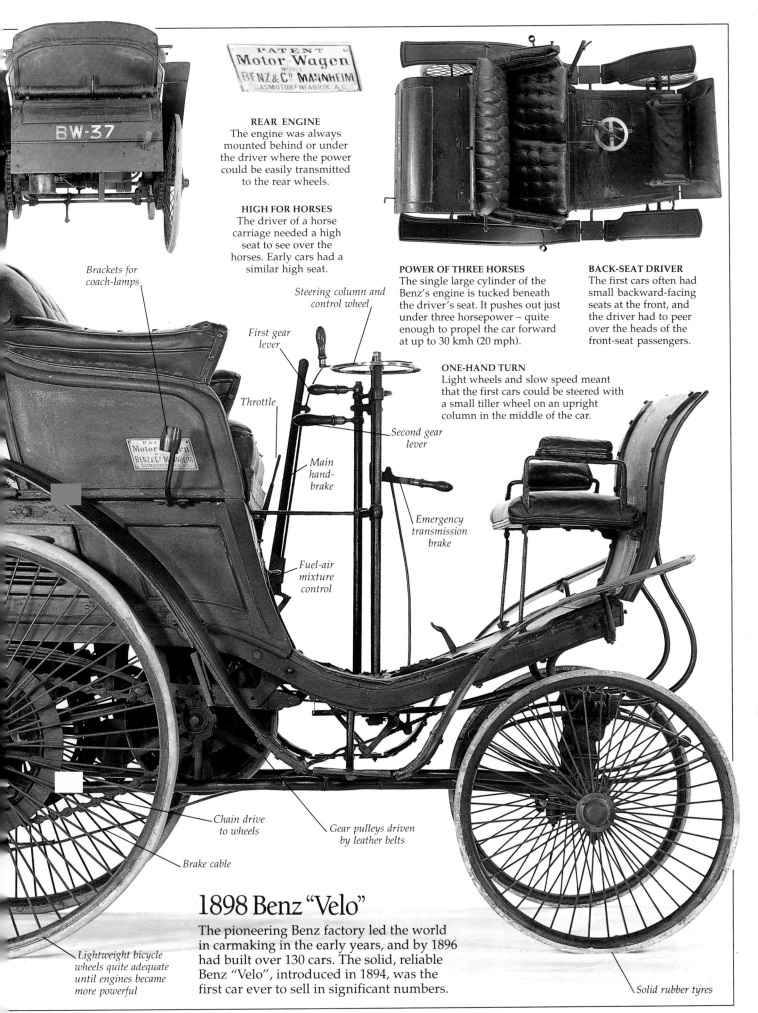

PATENT
Motor-Wagen
BENZ & Co. MANNHEIM
GASMOTORENFABRIK, A.G.

REAR ENGINE
The engine was always mounted behind or under the driver where the power could be easily transmitted to the rear wheels.

HIGH FOR HORSES
The driver of a horse carriage needed a high seat to see over the horses. Early cars had a similar high seat.

Brackets for coach-lamps

Steering column and control wheel

First gear lever

POWER OF THREE HORSES
The single large cylinder of the Benz's engine is tucked beneath the driver's seat. It pushes out just under three horsepower – quite enough to propel the car forward at up to 30 kmh (20 mph).

BACK-SEAT DRIVER
The first cars often had small backward-facing seats at the front, and the driver had to peer over the heads of the front-seat passengers.

ONE-HAND TURN
Light wheels and slow speed meant that the first cars could be steered with a small tiller wheel on an upright column in the middle of the car.

Throttle

Second gear lever

Main hand-brake

Emergency transmission brake

Fuel-air mixture control

Chain drive to wheels

Gear pulleys driven by leather belts

Brake cable

1898 Benz "Velo"

The pioneering Benz factory led the world in carmaking in the early years, and by 1896 had built over 130 cars. The solid, reliable Benz "Velo", introduced in 1894, was the first car ever to sell in significant numbers.

Lightweight bicycle wheels quite adequate until engines became more powerful

Solid rubber tyres

The pioneers

By 1900, CARS WERE LOOKING MORE LIKE CARS and less like horse carriages. The pioneering cars were difficult to start, and even more difficult to drive. But each year new ideas made the car a more practical and useful machine. In France, carmakers such as Panhard Levassor, De Dion Bouton, and Renault were especially inventive. It was Panhard who thought of putting the engine at the front and, in 1895, built the first saloon car. Renault championed the idea of a shaft, rather than a chain, to drive the rear wheels. In the early 1900s, the French runabouts were by far the most popular cars in Europe. Everywhere, though, the car was making progress. In the United States, where the Duryea brothers had made the first successful American car in 1893, little cars such as the famous Oldsmobile Curved Dash were selling by the thousand. In Britain in 1900, 23 cars completed a 1000-mile (1600 km) run from London to Scotland and back.

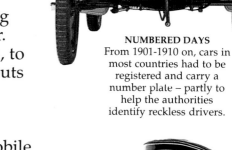

NUMBERED DAYS
From 1901-1910 on, cars in most countries had to be registered and carry a number plate – partly to help the authorities identify reckless drivers.

WOOD WORKS
The bodywork of early automobiles was made almost entirely of wood, often by a traditional coachbuilder, and painted just like old coachwork.

TOOL ROOM
Since few people expected to drive far in the pioneering days, most cars had very little space for luggage – the boot was usually filled with tools and spare parts!

Boot

INFERNAL MACHINES
The arrival of the first cars in country towns and villages created quite a stir. But they were not always welcome, for they scared horses and threw up thick clouds of dust.

"GET OUT AND GET UNDER!"
Breakdowns marred many a day out in early motor cars – and even inspired a famous music hall song. Here the mechanic has removed the front seat – probably to get at the troublesome drive gear. But such mishaps were already less common in 1903 than they had been five years earlier.

Coach-type leaf spring

KEEPING CLEAN
One early concession to comfort on the motor car was the addition of mudguards around the wheels to protect passengers from dirt thrown up off the roads.

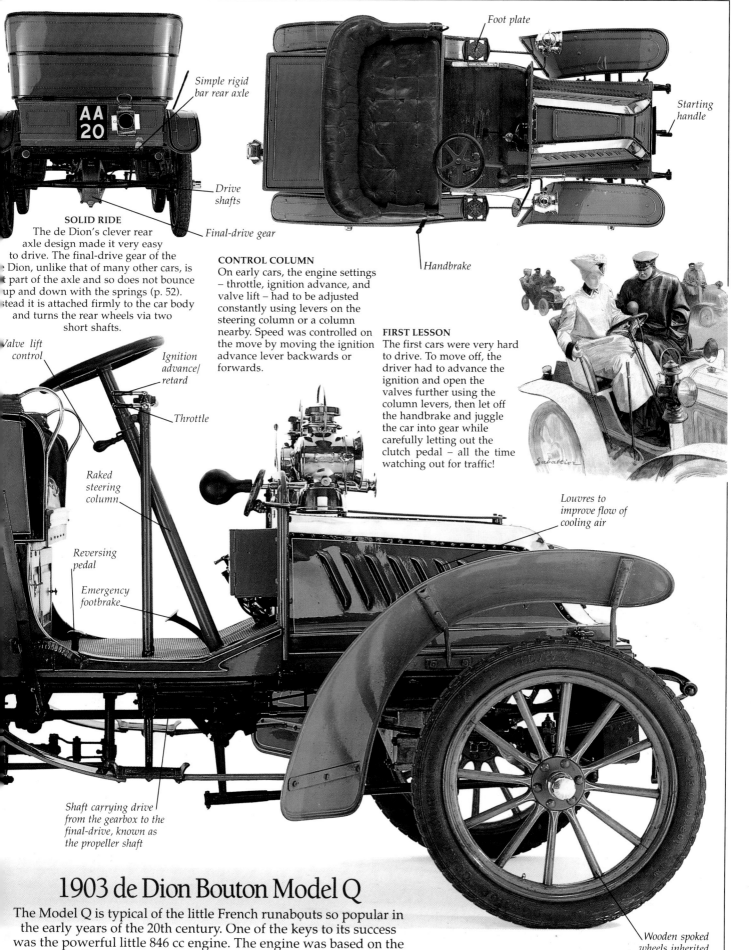

Simple rigid bar rear axle

AA 20

Drive shafts

Final-drive gear

SOLID RIDE
The de Dion's clever rear axle design made it very easy to drive. The final-drive gear of the de Dion, unlike that of many other cars, is not part of the axle and so does not bounce up and down with the springs (p. 52). Instead it is attached firmly to the car body and turns the rear wheels via two short shafts.

Foot plate

Starting handle

Handbrake

CONTROL COLUMN
On early cars, the engine settings – throttle, ignition advance, and valve lift – had to be adjusted constantly using levers on the steering column or a column nearby. Speed was controlled on the move by moving the ignition advance lever backwards or forwards.

FIRST LESSON
The first cars were very hard to drive. To move off, the driver had to advance the ignition and open the valves further using the column levers, then let off the handbrake and juggle the car into gear while carefully letting out the clutch pedal – all the time watching out for traffic!

Valve lift control

Ignition advance/ retard

Throttle

Raked steering column

Reversing pedal

Emergency footbrake

Louvres to improve flow of cooling air

Shaft carrying drive from the gearbox to the final-drive, known as the propeller shaft

Wooden spoked wheels inherited from the horse-cart

1903 de Dion Bouton Model Q

The Model Q is typical of the little French runabouts so popular in the early years of the 20th century. One of the keys to its success was the powerful little 846 cc engine. The engine was based on the old Daimler, but was designed to run twice as fast.

Warning signals

EARLY CARS were hard to control – and even harder to stop. Yet the roads were full of hazards – potholes, sharp bends, steep hills, and stray animals. Even the shortest outing in a car rarely passed without incident. Road signs were put up to warn drivers of coming dangers, but unwary animals and pedestrians were all too often hit or forced to leap out of the way by speeding motor cars. To protect people from these "scorchers", horns and other warning devices were made compulsory and frantic tooting soon became a familiar sound on rural roads.

Perforated dirt-cover

DRIVER: "HE MIGHT HAVE KILLED US!"
The recklessness of some motorists – summed up in this cartoon – meant that accidents were common.

Mounting bracket

WARNING BELL *below*
A popular alternative to the horn, which left the driver's hands free to control the car, was this American foot-operated gong. Called the "Clarion Bell", it made a very unlikely sound for a motor car.

Foot switch

Resonator

TRUMPET HORN *above*
Common on early cars was the bulb-blown trumpet horn – not so different from the mouth-blown horns used on the old stage coaches. This 1903 Mercedes horn has a long tube so that the horn can be mounted towards the front of the car.

Air bulb

STRAIGHT TUBE
Not all old horns were elaborate. Horns such as this French Simplicorn, originally fitted to the dashboard of a 1903 De Dion Bouton, were simple but effective.

...ET SOUND *left*
...etimes called a
...ar-pot", this rare
...n dating from 1911
...a distinctive, fluty
... The perforated
...piece prevents dirt
...ng in. It also means
...horn is effective
...a at speed, when
...headwind may
...oo much for
...r horns.

OUT OF CONTROL *left*
Farmer: "Pull up you fool! This horse is bolting!" Motorist: "So is the car!" This cartoon shows how much difficulty early drivers had in controlling their machines – and why they were so unpopular with horse riders and carters alike.

SPEED LIMIT *right*
Motor cars have been restricted by speed limits right from the start. In Britain, there was the "Red Flag" Act of 1865 which required that all cars have two drivers, while a third walked in front waving a red flag. The act was repealed in 1896, but new speed limits were soon imposed everywhere.

...OF MY WAY! *above*
...e hands of many an
...gant motorist, horns
... not just warning
...als but devices for
...ering pedestrians off
...oad. Fearsome boa
...trictor horns like this
... sold as accessories. Such
...s were usually made of brass
...often decorated with jewelled
...and red jutting tongues.

Mounting bracket

Translucent indicator hand

Metal tongue

HAND SIGNALS *right*
As cars became more and more common on the road, so drivers began to signal their intentions to other road users by standard hand signals. Those shown here mean, from top to bottom: I am stopping; I am slowing down; you may overtake; I am turning to the left; I am turning to the right.

Swivelling wrist

HAND-OUT *right*
For those with money, there were soon all kinds of weird and wonderful motoring gadgets on sale. One strange device is this cable-operated hand, dating from 1910 – long before flashing indicators were developed. It clipped on to the car door and the driver could turn a knob on the dashboard to mimic all the hand signals. It also lit up at night.

Rubber-lined, flexible brass tube

AIR POWER *below left*
Modern horns are electrically operated, and the sound comes from a diaphragm vibrated by an electro-magnet. In this air horn, compressed air vibrates the diaphragm especially loudly.

Diaphragm

Electric terminal

...ompressor

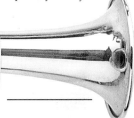

Coachbuilt splendour

Elegant ladies and their uniformed chauffeurs became the subject of many a romantic story

As CARS BECAME CHEAPER and more popular, so the rich wanted more and more exclusive auto-mobiles. The luxury cars of the pre-war years were made with the best technology and the best craftsmanship. No expense was spared, and these luxury autos – Hispano-Suizas, Benzs, Delauney-Belvilles, and Rolls-Royces – were built to standards rarely seen again in carmaking. Interiors were furnished with velvet and brocade, fine leather and thick pile carpets. Bodies were made precisely to the customers' requirements by the finest coachbuilders. The engines were large, powerful, and smooth-running. But they were cars not for the rich to drive, but to be driven in, by professional chauffeurs or motormen.

FASHIONABLE MOTORING
Rich ladies did not expect to drive; they simply wanted to be driven in style. One said, "I am not concerned in the least with the motor. I leave (that) to Monsieur Chauffeur. My only interest is in the interior."

OPEN CHOICE
Open tourers were often preferred to tall, closed limousines which swayed alarmingly on corners. This one is in style known as "Roi des Belges", af the body made for the King of Belgium's 1901 Panhard.

Folding "Cape-cart" hood

Folding windscreen for rear seat passenger

COVER UP
Motorists were quite happy with an open tourer providing it had "a light Cape-cart hood on the back to keep the dust out and set up in case of heavy rain".

Air-filled "pneumatic" tyre

Brake drum

HOUSEHOLD SWITCHES
Even on luxury cars, many body parts were not specially made, but adapted from other uses. Electrical switches were like those used in the home. The dial is an ammeter showing electrical current.

Toolbox

Ratc for ho brake descen hil

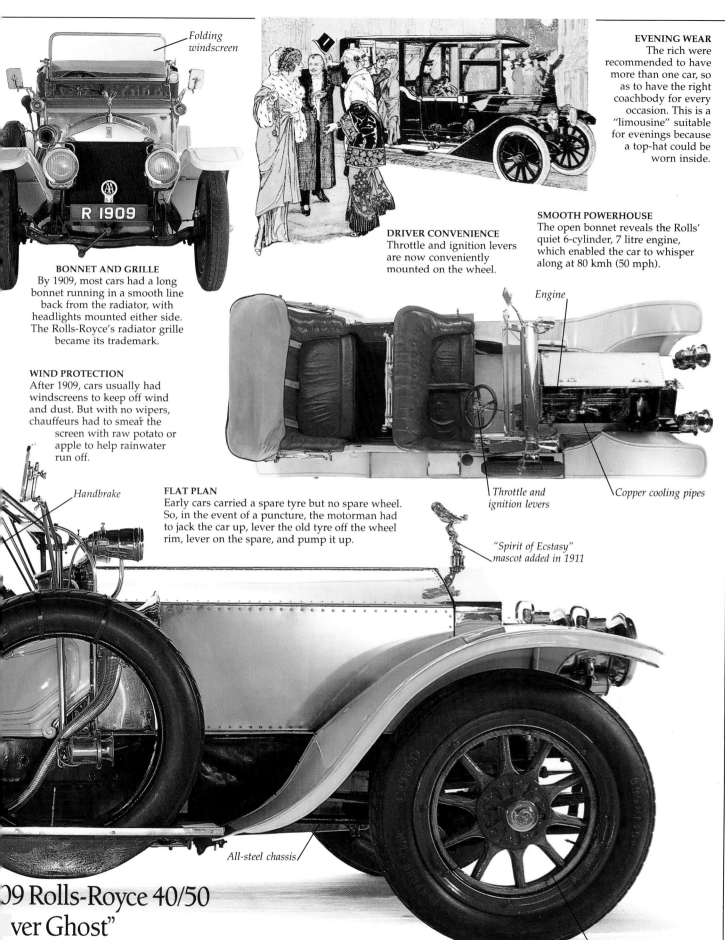

Folding windscreen

EVENING WEAR
The rich were recommended to have more than one car, so as to have the right coachbody for every occasion. This is a "limousine" suitable for evenings because a top-hat could be worn inside.

DRIVER CONVENIENCE
Throttle and ignition levers are now conveniently mounted on the wheel.

SMOOTH POWERHOUSE
The open bonnet reveals the Rolls' quiet 6-cylinder, 7 litre engine, which enabled the car to whisper along at 80 kmh (50 mph).

BONNET AND GRILLE
By 1909, most cars had a long bonnet running in a smooth line back from the radiator, with headlights mounted either side. The Rolls-Royce's radiator grille became its trademark.

WIND PROTECTION
After 1909, cars usually had windscreens to keep off wind and dust. But with no wipers, chauffeurs had to smear the screen with raw potato or apple to help rainwater run off.

Engine

Handbrake

FLAT PLAN
Early cars carried a spare tyre but no spare wheel. So, in the event of a puncture, the motorman had to jack the car up, lever the old tyre off the wheel rim, lever on the spare, and pump it up.

Throttle and ignition levers

Copper cooling pipes

"Spirit of Ecstasy" mascot added in 1911

09 Rolls-Royce 40/50
ver Ghost"

n Charles Rolls and Henry Royce made their first car in 1906, it soon me known as "the best car in the world" because of its sheer quality. Ghost-quietness and a shiny aluminium body earned it the name "Silver Ghost".

All-steel chassis

Wooden-spoked wheel

The open road

Owning a motor car provided every reason for dressing up and getting equipped for touring. Indeed, protective clothing was vital the open cars of the pioneer era. Not only was there rain and cold t contend with but, worst of all, the dreadful dust thrown up by dry dirt roads. Motorists would often come home covered from head to foot in a thick layer of muck. At first, clothes were adapted from riding and yachting and oth outdoor pursuits. But before long a huge variety of specialist motoring clothes was on sale. Some were practical and sensible; others clearly for show. A motorist could easily spend as much on a motoring wardrobe as on a new car. Yet the pleasures of the open road made all the little hardships and expense worthwhile, and touring became highly fashionable.

Nose-swivel to ensure good fit

Orange tint to reduce road glare

Dust-flap for ears

THE RIGHT GEAR
Goggles and head-gear were vital in an open car with no windscreen. At first, peaked caps (right) were popular with the fashion-conscious; serious drivers preferred helmet and goggles (left and above). But soon most drivers were wearing helmets – with built-in visors, ear muffs and even "anti-collision protectors".

DRESSED TO DRIVE *above*
Here are just some of the many styles of early motoring wear. The woman's "beekeeper" bonnet was very popular with fashionable ladies for keeping dust off the face and hair. Thick fur coats were usually made from Russian sable, ocelot, and beaver at huge expense.

Copper body to conduct heat

HOT FOOT
Sitting in an open car on a winter's day could be bitterly cold. Many a passenger must have been grateful for a footwarmer like this, which could be filled with hot water before setting out. Foot muffs and "putties" (leggings) also helped keep out the cold.

HANDY WEAR
The driver's hands would soon get very cold and dirty on the controls. So a good pair of gloves – preferably gauntlets – was essential. Gauntlets were usually fur-lined leather, just like modern motorcycle gloves.

Heatproof felt

TEA BAG *left*
With few roadside cafés, taking your own tea with you was a necessity – and all part of the great adventure of motoring. Since the journey could take hours, and you could be stranded anywhere, it was worth doing it properly. So motorists paid out for elaborate and beautifully made tea baskets like this one in leather and silver. They often came with a matching lunch basket.

Tea box

Combined kettle and teapot

PICNIC BY THE SEA
While only the rich could afford a car, motoring picnics tended to be lavish. The luxury shops hired out fine cutlery and glass, and supplied hampers filled with high-class food, including whole roast chickens and champagne.

Paraffin stove to heat water   *Matchbox*

THE JOYS OF MOTORING *left*
Car advertisements made the most of the pleasures of fast motoring through lovely countryside. This is a typical picture of an average 1920s American saloon, a six-cylinder Essex.

WHERE NEXT? *right*
Getting lost became a regular hazard for pioneer motorists on tour. Signposts were then few and far between. One dirt road looked much like another. And there was no coachman on hand to guide the motorist safely home. Sets of the new, detailed road maps that quickly appeared in the shops became as vital to the auto-tourist as a set of spanners.

Complete set of road maps in leather index case, from the 1920s

Mass-production

CARS WERE THE TOYS OF THE RICH in the early days. But it wa[s] Detroit farmboy Henry Ford's dream to build "a motor car for the great multitude – a car so low in price that no man making a good salary will be unable to own one". When he finally realized h[is] dream, with the launch of the Model T Ford in 1908, the effect was revolutionary. The T meant people barely able to afford a horse and buggy could buy a car. In 1908, less than 200,000 people in the USA owne[d] cars; five years later 250,000 owned Model Ts alone. By 1930, over 15 million Ts had been sold. The key to Ford's success was mass-production. By using huge teams of men working systematically to build huge numbers of cars, he could sell them all very cheaply. Indeed, the more he sold, the cheaper they became.

BOLT-ON WING
A simple mounting bracket slots through the hole and bolts on to the mudguard.

Simple hinged half-door

Wood-framed body tub

Pneumatic tyre

Wooden spoked

Body-mounting bracket

DROP-ON BODY
The wooden framed body tub (here missing its seat cushion or "squab") was made on another production line then lowered on the chassis at the right moment.

Exhaust pipe

Back-axle and final-drive gear

Frame for fold-down roof

Buttoned leather upholstery

Pressed steel body panel

ROLLING CHASSIS
The wheels were fitted early in production so that the chassis could be easily moved.

The production line

Before Ford, complete cars were built by small teams of men. In the Ford factory, each worker added just one small component, as partly assembled cars were pulled rapidly past on the production line.

Rear mudguard

HENRY FORD AND SON
The principles Ford used to make the
[Mo]del T are used in motor manufacture
[to]day. Modern assembly lines
use robots to build cars more
[qu]ickly, cheaply, and accurately.
But the idea of assembling
components on a moving
production line remains.

[KIT]Y BIT
[It's e]asy to see how the Model T
[takes] shape from its individual
[comp]onents. Mudguards, running
[board], and sill all bolt together to
[form] one side of the car, and are
[boltl]ed directly on to the chassis.

STANDARD VARIATIONS
One of the things that
made the Model T so cheap
was its standardized body.
At the time, most car
bodies were built
separately by specialist
coachbuilders; the
Model T's was made
right on the Ford
production line. So Ts
could not be tailor-made
to suit individual
customers' requirements.
Instead, Ford offered a
limited variety of
alternative body styles.

1909 Phaeton

1911 Runabout

1916 Doctor's coupé

1927 Tourer

*Outrigger
to support
bodywork*

Fuel tank

STAMP COLLECTION
Before mass-production,
this panel would have been
hand-made. Ford used
machines to stamp it out in
a fraction of the time.

*2898cc engine
giving top
speed of 65
kmh (40 mph)*

Gearbox

Bonnet

*Radiator surround
to support bonnet*

Handbrake

Radiator

TOUGH TIN
The T's chassis appeared
fragile, earning it the nickname
"Tin Lizzie". But it was made
from vanadium steel, which
proved very strong.

*[H]and
[st]eering*

RUNNING REPAIRS
Simplicity and
practicality were the
keynotes in the T; its
bonnet folded back or
lifted right off for easy
access to the engine.

Ford Model T c1912
The cheap, tough and thoroughly reliable
Model T put America, and much of the
world, on the roads for the first
time – and earned the affection of
two whole generations of
American families.

Sill

Front mudguard

[R]unning board

ONLY ONE COLOUR
Ford claimed that his car was
available in "any colour you like, so long as
it's black". This meant painting was cheap and
simple. Later models came in other colours.

Supercharged power

In the 1920s, many motorists owned powerful new "sports" cars – cars made purely for the pleasure of driving fast. The sports cars of the 1920s had huge engines and devices such as superchargers to give them an extra turn of speed. A few cars, including the Duesenberg J and the Bentley, could top 160 kmh (100 mph). Sports cars like these often had an impressive racing pedigree, for manufacturers were aware of the publicity to be won from success in motor racing. Alfa Romeo, Buga Bentley, Chevrolet, and Duesenberg all earned their reputations on the race track. And technical innovations made to win races were quickly put into cars for the ordinary motorist; the Bentley sold to t public was little, if any, different from its racing counterpart.

ONLY THE BRAVEST
A Delage speeds above the famous red line at Montlhery near Paris. To run so high on the banking, cars had to go over 150 kmh (90 mph).

BACK-SEAT RACERS
To bridge the gap between road cars and racing cars, some races in the 1920s were closed to all but four-seater tourers. The famous 24-hour event at Le Mans in France was such a race – which is why this Bentley had a back seat.

SINGLE EXIT
The Bentley has only one front door, for the benefit of co-driver. On the driver's side, there is simply a dip in the bodywork to make the outside handbrake easy to reach.

1930 Bentley 4.5 li supercharg

A series of sensational victories i Le Mans 24-hour races in 1924, 1927, 1929, and 1930 made the big Bentleys legen

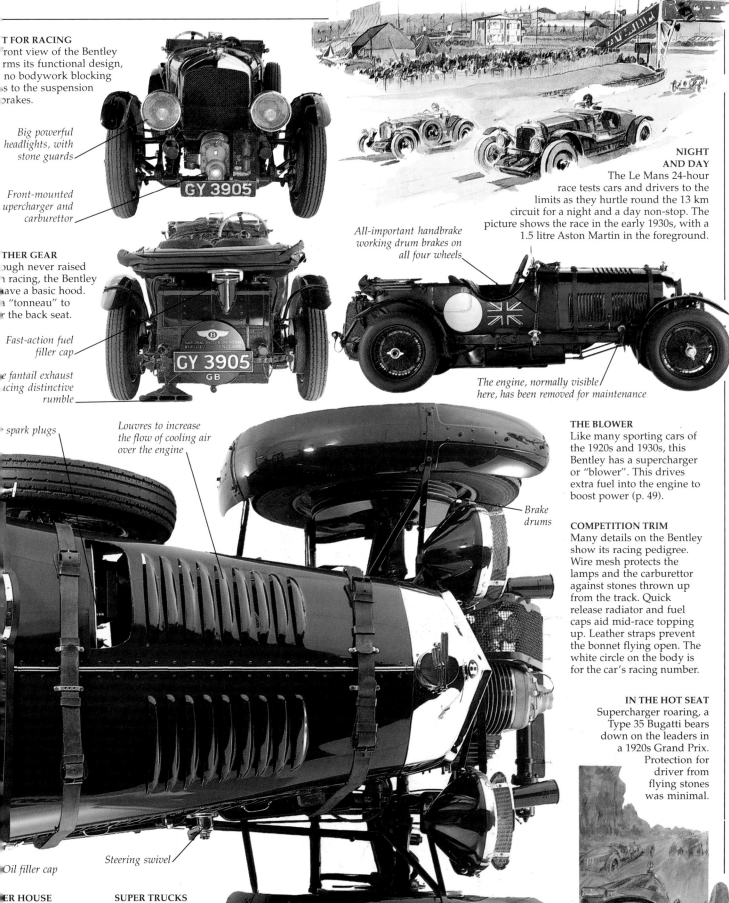

T FOR RACING
ront view of the Bentley
rms its functional design,
no bodywork blocking
s to the suspension
rakes.

Big powerful headlights, with stone guards

Front-mounted supercharger and carburettor

THER GEAR
ugh never raised
racing, the Bentley
ave a basic hood.
a "tonneau" to
the back seat.

Fast-action fuel filler cap

e fantail exhaust cing distinctive rumble

spark plugs

Louvres to increase the flow of cooling air over the engine

Brake drums

Oil filler cap

Steering swivel

ER HOUSE
rb engines, built in
4.5, 6.5, and 8 litre
ons, made the
eys very quick. The
charged 4.5 litre
els could top
mh (125 mph).

SUPER TRUCKS
The speed, size, and
rugged, no-nonsense
looks of the Bentleys
provoked Italian car-
designer Ettore Bugatti
to describe them as "the
world's fastest lorries".

NIGHT AND DAY
The Le Mans 24-hour race tests cars and drivers to the limits as they hurtle round the 13 km circuit for a night and a day non-stop. The picture shows the race in the early 1930s, with a 1.5 litre Aston Martin in the foreground.

All-important handbrake working drum brakes on all four wheels

The engine, normally visible here, has been removed for maintenance

THE BLOWER
Like many sporting cars of the 1920s and 1930s, this Bentley has a supercharger or "blower". This drives extra fuel into the engine to boost power (p. 49).

COMPETITION TRIM
Many details on the Bentley show its racing pedigree. Wire mesh protects the lamps and the carburettor against stones thrown up from the track. Quick release radiator and fuel caps aid mid-race topping up. Leather straps prevent the bonnet flying open. The white circle on the body is for the car's racing number.

IN THE HOT SEAT
Supercharger roaring, a Type 35 Bugatti bears down on the leaders in a 1920s Grand Prix. Protection for driver from flying stones was minimal.

Lighting the way

Night driving today is relatively safe and easy, thanks to t[he] power and efficiency of modern car lighting. But in the early days, lighting was so poor that few motorists ventured out o[n] the road after dark. The lights on the first cars were candle lamps inherited from horse-drawn carriages. They were so dim that they did little more than warn other road users of the car's presence. Special car ligh[ts] were soon developed, running first on oil or acetylene gas then electricity. Yet for many years lights were considered as luxury accessories. It was not until the 1930s that bright electric lights were fitted as standard on most cars.

"Pie-crust" chimney top

MIDNIGHT OIL
Robust lamps purpose-built for cars, burning oil or petrol, were in widespread use by 1899. The popular Lucas King of the Road "motor carriage lamp" (right) had a small red lens to the rear; separate tail lights like the Miller (below) were not made compulsory until much later.

Chi[mney]

Fron[t] cat[ch] allow [a]ccess for lig[hting] the [wick]

Oil reservoir

Red-stained glass lens

Wick adjuster

Oil reservoir

Candle wick holder

Spring-loaded candle holder

WAX WORKS *left*
The pioneers' cars had brackets for candle carriage lamps. Carriage lamps were beautifully made, and a spring pushed the candle up as it burned down. But dim candles were no good at all for driving. Even a slight breeze blew out the flame, while the jolting of the car shook the lamps to pieces. Candle lamps did serve a purpose, however. If the car was stranded after nightfall by a breakdown, they illuminated the immobile vehicle.

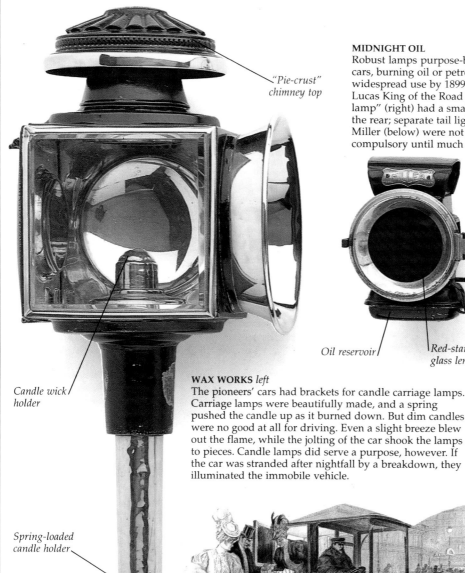

A NIGHT OUT *left*
In streetlit cities, it was just possible to drive after dark on candle lamps. This advert promotes the attractions of arriving for an evening gala by car. A troublesome horse in the background completes the illusion.

BIG MATCH
Lighting a candle lamp or even an o[il] lamp on a windy [day] was a tricky busin[ess]. Special strongly flaring "motor matches", made "[for] use on motor cars [and] launches", made l[ife] for the motorist a [little] less difficult.

ELECTRIC DREAMS
By the 1930s, electric lights were fitted as standard on most cars, and headlights – up to 33 cm (13 in) across – were included in the car's overall styling.

LIGHT RELIEF
While road surfaces were poor and bulbs still large and fragile, bulb breakages were frequent. The wise motorist always carried a full set of spares.

Early double element "dipping" headlight bulb

OLD FLAME
The first acetylene car lamps appeared around 1898. They needed constant maintenance and occasionally exploded. But, for those who could afford them, they were much better than candles and oil, giving a steady white light, bright enough for driving slowly by. They remained in use until 1939.

...ylene ...ly ...ster

WIRED FOR THE NIGHT
Electric car lights were first made as early as 1901. However, only in the 1920s, once cars had powerful generators, did electricity begin to take over from acetylene and night driving become practical for the first time. Electric lights have improved a lot in power and reliability since then, but few modern units match the elegant simplicity of those made by Stephen Grebel in the 1920s (below).

Bulb holder supports

...ney

Acetylene gas burner

Glass "Mangin" mirror curved to reflect parallel beam

Domed glass front

Magnifying lens

Bulb pointing backwards towards the reflector

Power supply

Swivelling headlights

GAS SUPPLY
A familiar feature of acetylene lamps was the constant hissing of the gas generator as water dripped steadily on to solid carbide. The carbide fizzed as the water made contact, giving off a stream of acetylene gas. Sometimes the gas was made in the lamp itself; more often it was piped from a separate canister (below). New carbide had to be added every four hours or so.

...as ...ylene lamp

Window to show light sideways

LIGHT ALL AROUND
The forerunners of modern parking lights, electric lights like this were often mounted on the side of cars in the 1920s. Front, rear and side lenses gave all round visibility.

Headlight dipping lever

A QUICK DIP
Once headlights became bright enough to dazzle oncoming drivers, various ideas for interrupting the beam were tried. This one involved swivelling down ("dipping") the entire light.

Travelling in style

IF CRAFTSMANSHIP was sought after in the earliest cars and speed in the cars of the 1920s, then the 1930s was the era of styling. Beautiful body styling gave a car luxury appeal at a fraction of the cost of fine coachwork. A good design could be reproduced again and again on the production line. In the USA, manufacturers such as Auburn, Cord, Packard and others all made magnificent-looking cars in the 1930s – vast, extravagant cars that Hollywood stars posed beside, and Chicago gangsters drove. Such cars were not always well built, but with huge engines and elegant bodywork, they were usually fast and always glamorous.

Dist "V" fr spor

Elegant boat-shaped tail – with no bootlid

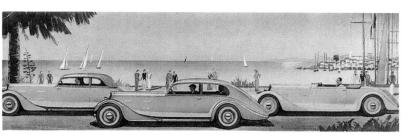

HEADING FOR THE SUN
The Depression years of the 1930s may have been hard for the poor, but for the rich and famous they were the golden days of grand touring or *grand routier*. Nothing followed a round of parties in Paris more naturally than a leisurely drive south to the French Riviera in a sleek open tourer like these Peugeots.

Entire metal tail section made in single pressing

Auburn insiginia

CAR FOR A STAR
You had to be someone special to be seen in a car like this. For a two-seater with minimal luggage space, it was massive – almost 6 m (over 17 ft) long, very tall and wide and clearly designed to impress. Film star Marlene Dietrich drove one.

Impractical but stylish "whitewall" tyres

Golf-club hatch

ESSENTIAL EQUIPMENT
The Auburn came complete with a locker for golf clubs and a radio as standard. The roof folded neatly down under the metal flap behind the passengers.

Radio a

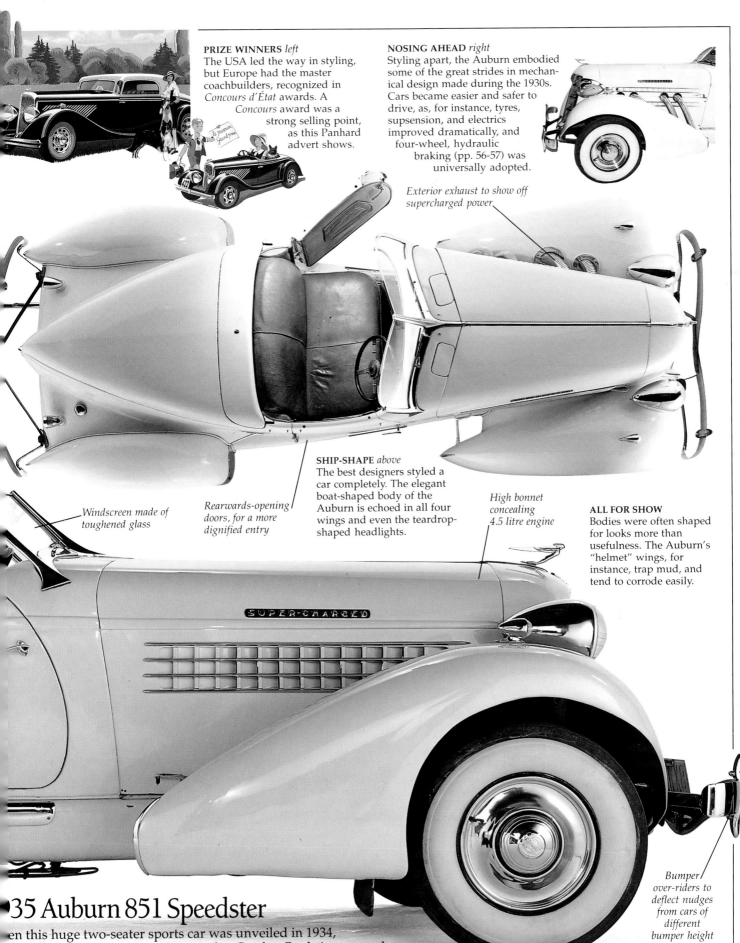

PRIZE WINNERS *left*
The USA led the way in styling, but Europe had the master coachbuilders, recognized in *Concours d'État* awards. A *Concours* award was a strong selling point, as this Panhard advert shows.

NOSING AHEAD *right*
Styling apart, the Auburn embodied some of the great strides in mechanical design made during the 1930s. Cars became easier and safer to drive, as, for instance, tyres, suspension, and electrics improved dramatically, and four-wheel, hydraulic braking (pp. 56-57) was universally adopted.

Exterior exhaust to show off supercharged power

SHIP-SHAPE *above*
The best designers styled a car completely. The elegant boat-shaped body of the Auburn is echoed in all four wings and even the teardrop-shaped headlights.

Windscreen made of toughened glass

Rearwards-opening doors, for a more dignified entry

High bonnet concealing 4.5 litre engine

ALL FOR SHOW
Bodies were often shaped for looks more than usefulness. The Auburn's "helmet" wings, for instance, trap mud, and tend to corrode easily.

SUPER-CHARGED

Bumper over-riders to deflect nudges from cars of different bumper height

35 Auburn 851 Speedster

en this huge two-seater sports car was unveiled in 1934, odywork – designed by master stylist Gordon Buehrig – caused nsation. The car was fast, too, powered by a supercharged eight-cylinder ine; every car came with a plaque certifying that it had been driven at over mph (160 kmh) by racing driver Ab Jenkins.

Family motoring

In the United States, many millions of people had already bought their own cars by 1930 – even though some may have had to sell their best chairs or mortgage their homes to pay for one. In the rest of the world, the price of a car was still beyond all but the wealthy.

Gradually, though, prices came down, and more and more middle-class families bought their first cars. The cars they bought were modest, inexpensive little saloons like the Austin Ten, the Opel Kadett and the Ford Y. With small engines and upright bodywork, they gave little in the way of performance. But roomy interiors provided enough space for both parents and children, and closed-in saloon cabins made them practical all-the-year-round transport.

OFF TO THE SEA
Trips to the seaside were fun for all the family. But it took time getting there. With four people aboard, this Austin Seven would travel no faster than 50 kmh (30 mph)!

MUMMY! CAN WE HAVE A CAR?
Carmakers aimed their cars, and adverts, squarely at the family. How many parents, burdened with babies and luggage, must have succumbed to this temptation to buy the Ford Y?

PLAY ROOM
Family cars of the 1930s were designed for maximum passenger space. The rear doors of the Austin Ten open backwards for easy access, and the back seat extends well over the rear wheels.

Winds
opens fo
air in su

Drum brakes on all four wheels

Lightweight wire wheels

1936 Austin Ten
With its modest performance, practical design, and low selling price, the Austin Ten is typical of the family cars o the 1930s. It is actually a more refined, bigger version of t famous "baby" Austin Seven, the first popular British car

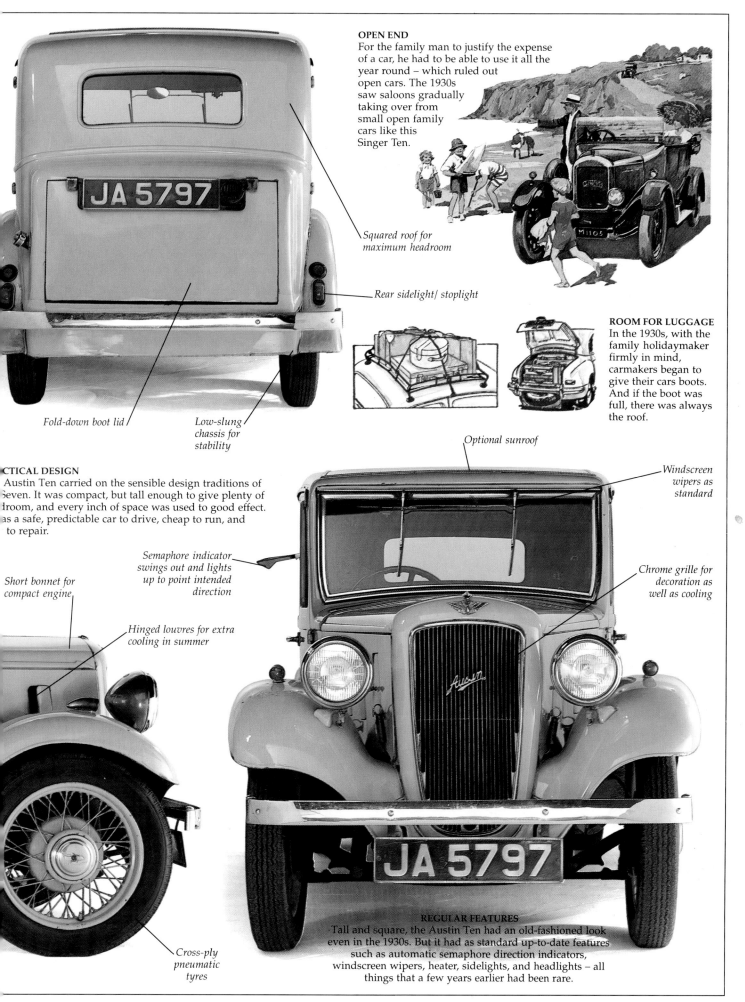

OPEN END
For the family man to justify the expense of a car, he had to be able to use it all the year round – which ruled out open cars. The 1930s saw saloons gradually taking over from small open family cars like this Singer Ten.

Squared roof for maximum headroom

Rear sidelight/ stoplight

ROOM FOR LUGGAGE
In the 1930s, with the family holidaymaker firmly in mind, carmakers began to give their cars boots. And if the boot was full, there was always the roof.

Fold-down boot lid

Low-slung chassis for stability

CTICAL DESIGN
Austin Ten carried on the sensible design traditions of Seven. It was compact, but tall enough to give plenty of droom, and every inch of space was used to good effect. as a safe, predictable car to drive, cheap to run, and to repair.

Optional sunroof

Windscreen wipers as standard

Semaphore indicator swings out and lights up to point intended direction

Short bonnet for compact engine

Hinged louvres for extra cooling in summer

Chrome grille for decoration as well as cooling

Cross-ply pneumatic tyres

REGULAR FEATURES
Tall and square, the Austin Ten had an old-fashioned look even in the 1930s. But it had as standard up-to-date features such as automatic semaphore direction indicators, windscreen wipers, heater, sidelights, and headlights – all things that a few years earlier had been rare.

High performance

THE 1950s SAW THE CREATION of a series of remarkable high performance cars. With the petrol rationing of the war years ending in 1950, designers started working on cars faster than anything seen before. Racing cars ha[d] been capable of speeds of over 220 kmh (140 m[ph]) before the war, but most road cars were much slower. In the early 1950s, however, a number o[f] expensive 220 kmh sports cars emerged from th[e] factories of big companies like Jaguar and Mercedes-Benz and specialists such as Porsche, Aston Martin, Maserati, and Ferrari. Designed with both road and track [in] mind, they were often called Grand Tourers, or GTs. But the GTs of the 1950s were very different from the big open Grand Tourers of the 1920s a[nd] 1930s. These cars were compact, usually closed-in, two-seater cars – cars not for leisurely motoring to the coast, but for scorching round winding roads at terrifying speeds. Many were winners on the racetrack, and could often match these performances on the road. Indeed, the road version of the Mercedes-Benz 300SL was a third more powerful than the racing prototype.

ROAD RACE
The famous Mille Miglia (1000 miles) was an endurance race for road cars run over 1600 km of winding public roads in Italy. The 300SL excelled several times in the race and, in 1955, won outright.

SPACE FRAME *below*
Designers of GTs sought to keep weight to a minimum. Mercedes succeeded by making the 300SL's unique chassis from tubular steel. The frame was light and strong – but its high sides were the reason for the "gullwing" doors.

1957 Mercedes-Benz 300SL "Gullwing"

With futuristic bodywork matched by advanced engineering that gave the car 230 kmh (144 mph) performance, the Mercedes-Benz 300SL was a true classic.

Hydraulic door supports

Stylized mudguard remnant

Quick-release "knock-off" wheel lock

Red leather lined passenger compartment

High sill be[...] of tube c[...]

WINGED ENTRY
300SL's upswinging
doors looked like the
wings of a seagull when
open. They were unique
at the time, but
absolutely necessary
because, with the
Mercedes's high sills,
conventional doors
would have been
impossible.

STYLING SENSATION
By 1955, few cars had
separate mudguards or
running boards; wings,
bonnet, and doors were part
of a unified whole. But the
300SL's flowing lines set
new standards in styling.

"Gullwing" doors

Bonnet humps to
allow for engine
clearance

Three-point
"Mercedes"
star

Wide tyres for
extra grip

ROAD AND TRACK
As with many sports cars of the 1950s,
there was little difference between
road and racing versions of the 300SL.
Indeed, road versions were so highly
tuned that they often overheated in
city traffic.

Essential ventilation
for sealed passenger
compartment

Curved, tinted
glass windscreen

Narrow,
reinforced
door pillars

NO LUGGAGE
The boot had
room for the
spare tyre only.

CLEAR DASH
The 300SL had just
two, not three, bars on
its steering wheel,
giving a clear view of
the instruments.

Body in silver,
Germany's official
racing colour

Short, fast-action
gearchange

Engine compartment containing
powerful six-cylinder, 3 litre, fuel-
injected engine.

Low bonnet
profile made
possible by tilting
engine sideways

American dream

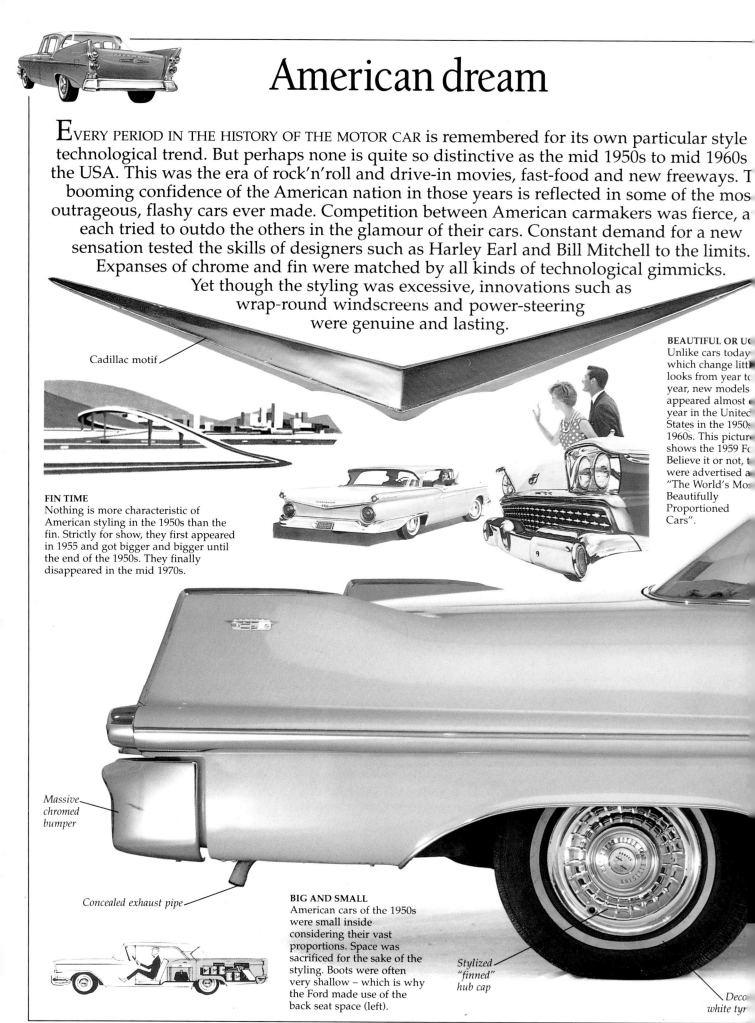

Every period in the history of the motor car is remembered for its own particular style technological trend. But perhaps none is quite so distinctive as the mid 1950s to mid 1960s the USA. This was the era of rock'n'roll and drive-in movies, fast-food and new freeways. T booming confidence of the American nation in those years is reflected in some of the mos outrageous, flashy cars ever made. Competition between American carmakers was fierce, a each tried to outdo the others in the glamour of their cars. Constant demand for a new sensation tested the skills of designers such as Harley Earl and Bill Mitchell to the limits. Expanses of chrome and fin were matched by all kinds of technological gimmicks. Yet though the styling was excessive, innovations such as wrap-round windscreens and power-steering were genuine and lasting.

Cadillac motif

FIN TIME
Nothing is more characteristic of American styling in the 1950s than the fin. Strictly for show, they first appeared in 1955 and got bigger and bigger until the end of the 1950s. They finally disappeared in the mid 1970s.

BEAUTIFUL OR U
Unlike cars today which change litt looks from year to year, new models appeared almost year in the Unitec States in the 1950 1960s. This pictur shows the 1959 Fc Believe it or not, t were advertised a "The World's Mo Beautifully Proportioned Cars".

Massive chromed bumper

Concealed exhaust pipe

BIG AND SMALL
American cars of the 1950s were small inside considering their vast proportions. Space was sacrificed for the sake of the styling. Boots were often very shallow – which is why the Ford made use of the back seat space (left).

Stylized "finned" hub cap

Deco white tyr

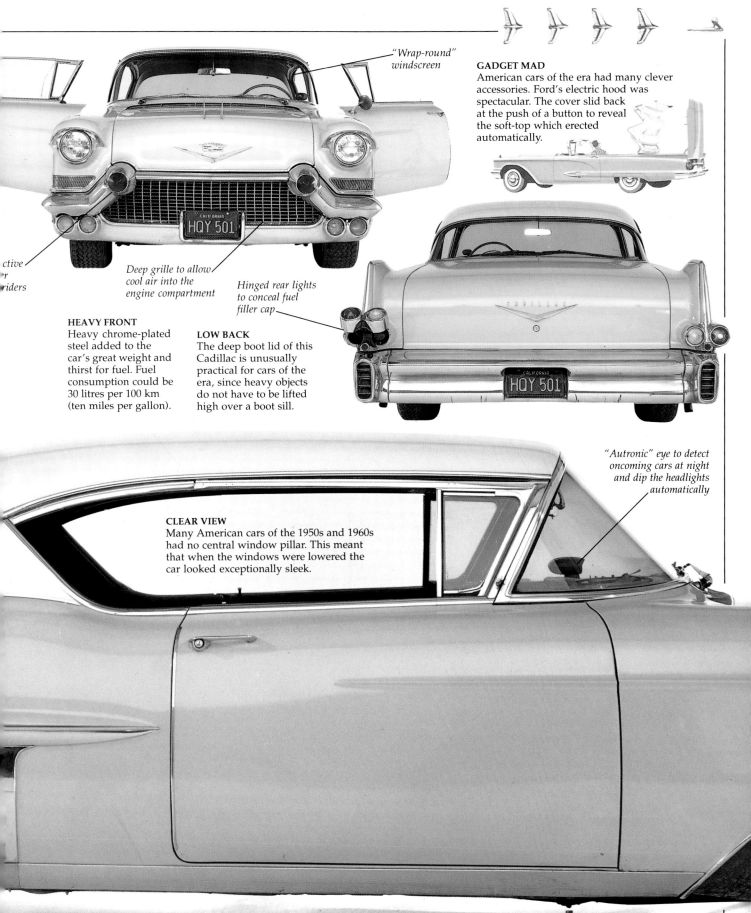

"Wrap-round" windscreen

GADGET MAD
American cars of the era had many clever accessories. Ford's electric hood was spectacular. The cover slid back at the push of a button to reveal the soft-top which erected automatically.

ctive
r
riders

Deep grille to allow cool air into the engine compartment

Hinged rear lights to conceal fuel filler cap

HEAVY FRONT
Heavy chrome-plated steel added to the car's great weight and thirst for fuel. Fuel consumption could be 30 litres per 100 km (ten miles per gallon).

LOW BACK
The deep boot lid of this Cadillac is unusually practical for cars of the era, since heavy objects do not have to be lifted high over a boot sill.

"Autronic" eye to detect oncoming cars at night and dip the headlights automatically

CLEAR VIEW
Many American cars of the 1950s and 1960s had no central window pillar. This meant that when the windows were lowered the car looked exceptionally sleek.

57 Cadillac Coupé de Ville

cal of American cars of the 1950s, the Coupé de Ville is almost
(18 ft) long and extravagantly finned and chromed. It also has
y advanced technical features, such as electrically winding
dows and reclining seats, and a smooth eight-cylinder engine.

POWER ASSISTANCE
Cadillacs, like most American luxury cars of the time, had "power-assisted" steering and braking – essential in such heavy cars.

Cars for the city

LITTLE MOUSE
The cheap and cheerful Fiat 500 "Topolino" (Little Mouse) became Italy's most popular car.

Iɴ ᴛʜᴇ 1950s, sᴍᴀʟʟ ᴄᴀʀs were cheaper than ever before. Cars such as the Volkswagen Beetle and the Renault 4 were so basic and inexpensive that they sold by the million. Indeed, so many cars were sold that city roads began to clog up. In London, the number of cars doubled; in Paris, *zones bleues* were imposed to restrict traffic; and in New York, they had to build massive urban freeways to relieve congestion. No wonder, then, that tiny "bubble" cars, such as the Italian Isetta, soon became all the rage – even though they were built essentially for economy rather than compactness. For a family, though, they were just a bit too small. One answer was the Mini, launched in 1959. A full-scale car in a minute package, the Mini was revolutionary. To make room for four adults in such a tiny car, engine and drive had to take up as little space as possible. So designer Alec Issigonis set the engine transversely (across the car), driving the front wheels. The idea worked so well that now nearly all family cars have the same layout.

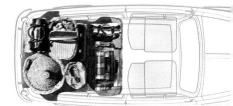

ITALIAN MINI
The tiny Fiat 500, launched in 1957, was ev smaller than the Mini and sold almost as v But passengers were cramped and the rear engined layout proved a dead end.

BUBBLING OVER
For a few years in the 1950s, tiny "bubble" cars like this Isetta were popular with city-dwellers. They had room for only two just three wheels, and a tiny, two-cylinder engine in the back. But they were short enough to fit endways into parking spaces – which is just a well, with the door at the front.

HIGH COMPRESSION
Fitting everything under the Mini's compact bonnet was a remarkable feat. Squeezed into tiny nose are all the engine components, coo system, gearbox and drive, steering gear, an the entire front suspension.

Space-rocket inspired bonnet mascot

Protective rubber over-rider

Carburettor

Chromed front apron

Chromed hubcaps popular in 1950s and 1960s

Side-mounted radiator keeps bonnet short

Tiny 25 cm (10 in) wheels saving valuable body space

Headlight dipswitch

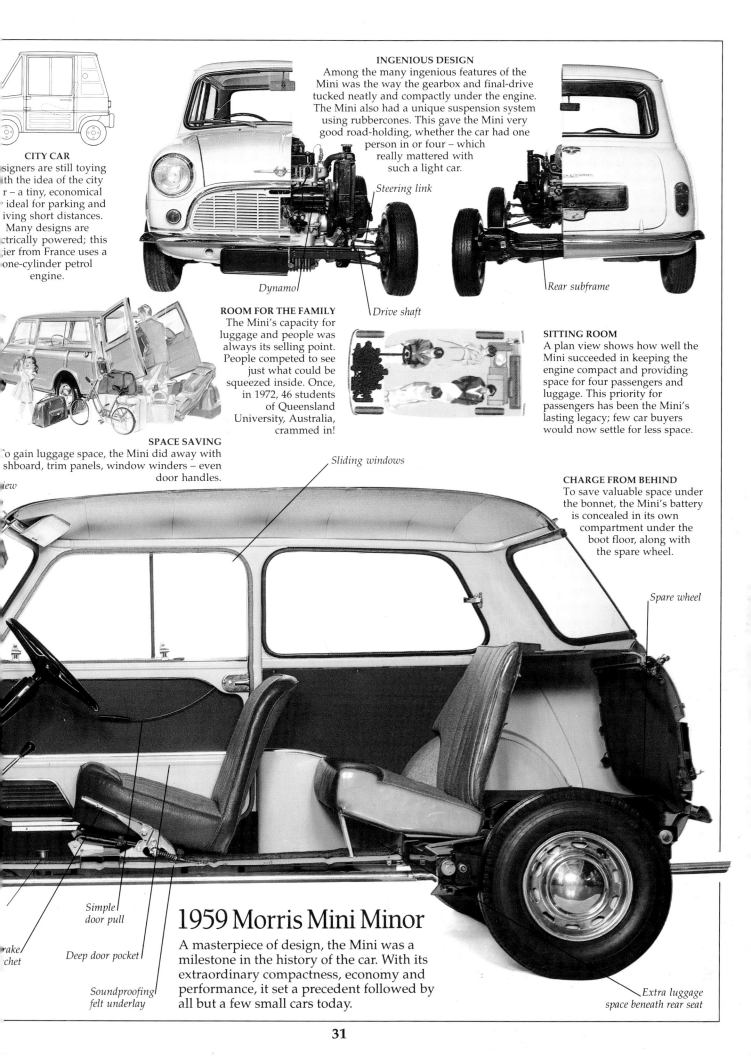

CITY CAR
[De]signers are still toying [wi]th the idea of the city [ca]r – a tiny, economical [car] ideal for parking and [dr]iving short distances. Many designs are [ele]ctrically powered; this [on]e from France uses a [??] one-cylinder petrol engine.

INGENIOUS DESIGN
Among the many ingenious features of the Mini was the way the gearbox and final-drive tucked neatly and compactly under the engine. The Mini also had a unique suspension system using rubbercones. This gave the Mini very good road-holding, whether the car had one person in or four – which really mattered with such a light car.

Steering link

Dynamo

Drive shaft

Rear subframe

ROOM FOR THE FAMILY
The Mini's capacity for luggage and people was always its selling point. People competed to see just what could be squeezed inside. Once, in 1972, 46 students of Queensland University, Australia, crammed in!

SITTING ROOM
A plan view shows how well the Mini succeeded in keeping the engine compact and providing space for four passengers and luggage. This priority for passengers has been the Mini's lasting legacy; few car buyers would now settle for less space.

SPACE SAVING
[T]o gain luggage space, the Mini did away with [da]shboard, trim panels, window winders – even door handles.

Sliding windows

CHARGE FROM BEHIND
To save valuable space under the bonnet, the Mini's battery is concealed in its own compartment under the boot floor, along with the spare wheel.

Spare wheel

Simple door pull

Deep door pocket

Soundproofing felt underlay

[br]ake [ra]tchet

1959 Morris Mini Minor
A masterpiece of design, the Mini was a milestone in the history of the car. With its extraordinary compactness, economy and performance, it set a precedent followed by all but a few small cars today.

Extra luggage space beneath rear seat

Racing car

FORMULA ONE RACING CARS are the ultimate speed machines, worlds apart from everyday road cars. Their open, one-seater bodies are made of new ultra-light materials and are so low slung they almost scrape the ground. The "fuselage" and wings are aerodynamically shaped to keep the wheels firmly on the road. Vast, wide tyres give extra grip at high speeds. And enormously powerful engines propel them around the track at speeds in excess of 300 kmh (190 mph). Motor racing is so fiercely competitive that designers are always trying new ideas to give their cars the edge in performance. But each car has to comply with strict rules laid down for Formula One cars, covering everything from the size of the fuel tank to the shape of the floorpan. To keep up with new developments, the rules must be updated almost every season, and the ingenuity of designers is tested to its limits as they try to adapt their designs to the new rules – and still beat their rivals.

FINISHING SCHOOL
The 500 cc events that started up in the 1950s have proved an ideal way into racing for many a budding Grand Prix driver.

ONE FOR THE ROAD
Pre-war racers looked little different from road cars.

DOUBLING UP
In the days before "slicks", cars w often fitted with double rear whee for extra traction in the hill-climb events popular until the mid 1950

AIR PRESSURE
Racing car bodies are not only streamlined to cut down air resistance; they are also shaped so that the air flowing over the car helps keep it on the road. The front and rear wings act like upside down aeroplane wings to push the wheels on to the ground.

GROUND EFFECT
In 1979, many racing cars had "skirts" almost touching the ground – so that, at high speed, air rushing under the car sucked it on to the ground. This "ground-effect" improved road-holding so much that skirts were soon banned because drivers were going too fast. Now cars have a "waist" to give the same effect.

Front coil springs and dampers mounted inboard to cut air resistance

Roll-bar to protect driver's head in a crash

Rear-view

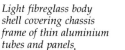

Sponsor's logo – Formula One racing is now such an expensive business that sponsorship is vital

"Skirt" to create a strong vacuum beneath the car when it is moving very fast

Light fibreglass body shell covering chassis frame of thin aluminium tubes and panels

Fuel tank inside body shell

Side panels to channel air over the wing

Quick-release, centre-lock wheels

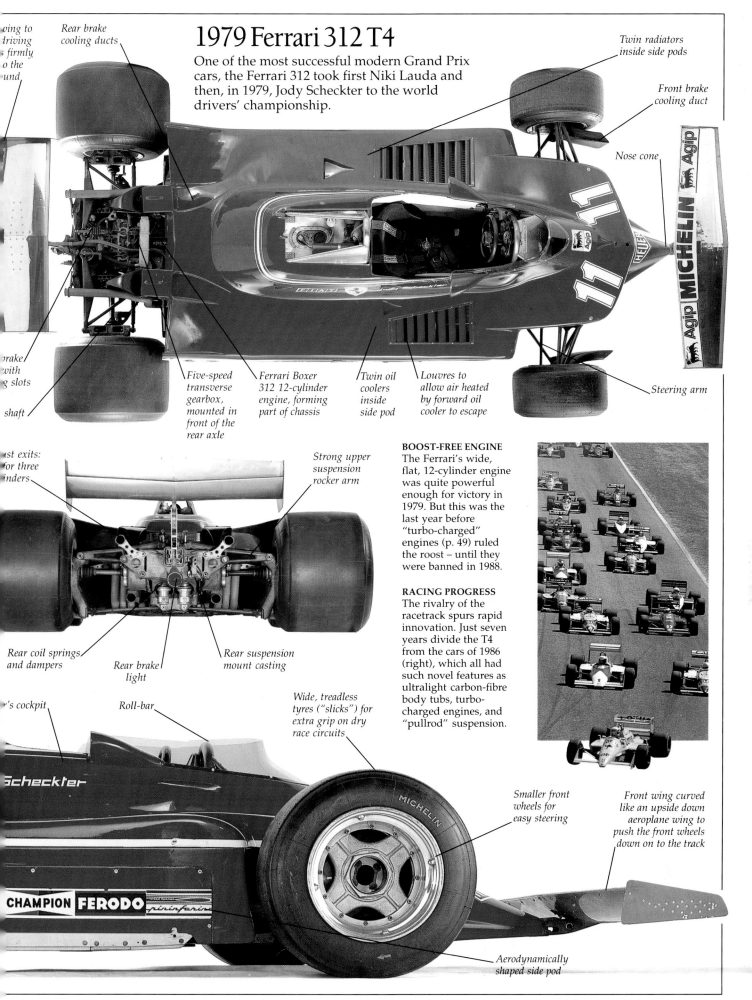

1979 Ferrari 312 T4

One of the most successful modern Grand Prix cars, the Ferrari 312 took first Niki Lauda and then, in 1979, Jody Scheckter to the world drivers' championship.

ving to driving firmly o the und

Rear brake cooling ducts

Twin radiators inside side pods

Front brake cooling duct

Nose cone

rake with g slots

shaft

Five-speed transverse gearbox, mounted in front of the rear axle

Ferrari Boxer 312 12-cylinder engine, forming part of chassis

Twin oil coolers inside side pod

Louvres to allow air heated by forward oil cooler to escape

Steering arm

st exits: or three nders

Strong upper suspension rocker arm

BOOST-FREE ENGINE
The Ferrari's wide, flat, 12-cylinder engine was quite powerful enough for victory in 1979. But this was the last year before "turbo-charged" engines (p. 49) ruled the roost – until they were banned in 1988.

RACING PROGRESS
The rivalry of the racetrack spurs rapid innovation. Just seven years divide the T4 from the cars of 1986 (right), which all had such novel features as ultralight carbon-fibre body tubs, turbo-charged engines, and "pullrod" suspension.

Rear coil springs and dampers

Rear brake light

Rear suspension mount casting

's cockpit

Roll-bar

Wide, treadless tyres ("slicks") for extra grip on dry race circuits

Smaller front wheels for easy steering

Front wing curved like an upside down aeroplane wing to push the front wheels down on to the track

Aerodynamically shaped side pod

Creating a car

FIRST SKETCH
Nearly every new car starts as a sketch on the designer's drawing board. The designer may draw dozens of these sketches before everyone is happy enough to proceed to a more detailed design drawing or "rendering".

ARCHITECT'S CAR
Designs that are too unconventional or impractical tend to be abandoned at an early stage – such as this design for a cheap city car proposed in the 1920s by the famous modern architect Le Corbusier.

CREATING A NEW CAR is a costly business, involving hundreds of people and years of intensive research. So a carmaker has to be confident that the car is going to sell before developing the concept far. Even before the designer draws the first rough sketch for the new car, the maker's requirements are laid down in detail in a "design brief" – including the car's precise dimensions, how many passenger it will carry, how many doors it will have, the engine layout and the transmission and much more besides. The route from the initial sketch to the finished car is a long one, and the design is subject to close scrutiny at all stages in the process. Several full-scale models are built – first usually from clay, then from fibre glass – and the design is constantl modified and refined. By the time the first production version rolls out of the factory, the car will work (and sell) perfectly – or so the carmaker hopes!

The interior is left blank since this mock-up is intended to show only the body styling

The clay is laid over a roughly shaped framework or "armature" of wood and foam slightly smaller than the finished model

Full-size clay mo

For the Fiat Panda, the designers were asked to come up with a car was light, roomy, cheap to run and immensely practical. After nume: design drawings and renderings, they built this full scale model of the b shell for their proposed car. It differs only in minor details from the real th

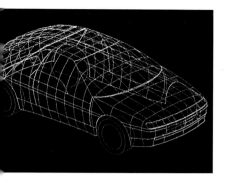

COMPUTER POWER
Computers are playing an increasingly important part in the design process. Most manufacturers now use Computer Aided Design (CAD) techniques, at least once the basic shape has been decided upon. Often a clay model of the design is scanned (right) to set up the computer with a complete set of profiles and contours (left). The computer can then be used to analyze such things as stresses in the body panel and to try the effect of changes at the touch of a button.

FUNCTIONAL APPROACH
Despite the clean lines, the front end is squarish – evidence that low cost and practicality were the priorities in design, not superb aerodynamics.

glossy
c film stuck
clay looks
ainy plastic
ings

Clay is applied warm and shaped to the contours of the design drawing by skilled clay modellers

MADE TO BE MADE
Car designers cannot afford to forget the possible cost of manufacturing their design. The simple shape of the body panels on this mock-up mean they should be economical to make.

Clay model may sometimes be used to create a mould for a fibre glass mock-up and broken up in the process

Clay bodywork painted to look like the real thing

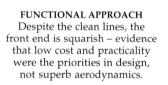

BLOWING IN THE WIND
Wind-tunnel testing has long been an important part of the design process. Hundreds of minor changes to the body profile may be made before the designers are finally satisfied that the car's "drag coefficient" is as low as they can practicallly get it.

Standardized "real" components need not be mocked-up in clay

The anatomy of a car

THE DAYS WHEN EVERY CAR had a strong chassis and separate coach-built body are long gone. Almost all cars today are of "unitary" construction, which means that chassis and body are made as a single unit – although some may also have a small "subframe" like the car here. Unitary bodywork makes a car both light and strong. It is also perfect for mass-production since it involves little more than welding together steel sheets stamped into shape by machines – all of which can be done by robots on the production line.

Rear "hatchback" door with double skin of pressed steel

Rear plastic bumper

Telescopic door stay

Body awaiting final coats of paint in chosen colour

Plastic trim panel to cover electrical wiring access

SAFETY SANDWICH
Car bodies are made so that the passengers sit inside a strong box which protects them in a crash. The front and back of the car, however, are "crumple zones", designed to collapse progressively and cushion the passengers from the impact.

PERFECT FIT
The right body proportions are all-important – the car must be small on the outside but big on the inside.

0.62
1.68
0.61
2.40
0.56
3.59

1.39
1.32
1.58

0.88
1.29

Plastic rear side window seal

PRESS ENTRANCE
By stamping doors out of two sheets or "skins" of steel, rather than making a separate frame, manufacturers can keep costs down.

Door hinges

ROBOT MADE
In many car factories, body production is fully automated. On this assembly line for the Rover 200, 22 robots apply over 1000 welds to each car.

STANDARD PRODUCT
To make body shells by robot, manufacturers have to install huge amounts of equipment, so they have to sell many identical cars.

STRONG POINT
The inner wing is strengthened to take the front suspension.

LASER ACCURACY
Each body is checked for inaccuracies in the "auto-gauging station". Laser beams detect the tiniest mistakes in panel fit.

PLASTIC PADDING
Plastic bumpers resist gentle knocks better than steel.

Plastic bumper

Inner wing

Radiator grille

Crushable bumper buffers

Coating applied by electrifying the body, a process called "cataphoresis"

Chrome treatment to reduce corrosive reactions

Bare steel

Degreased steel

Zinc phosphate rust treatment

Paint primer

Opaque finish

Matt paint and supergloss varnish

Zinc phosphate

Base coat and varnish

Coloured top coats

MULTI-COATED
To protect from rust, and to give it a good, hard-wearing finish, the bodywork has to be dipped and sprayed many times in paint and anti-corrosion treatments. Renault Five body panels get 15 different coats.

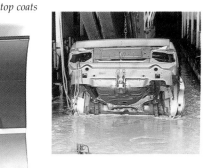

ZINCING FEELING
To protect the body against rust, it is immersed in a bath of zinc phosphate. The body is then electrified to make the phosphate stick to the metal.

Continued on next page

Continued from previous page

Moving parts

A small car like this has some 30,000 individual mechanical components. But each component goes to make up just a few basic systems, such as the fuel system, exhaust, suspension, brakes, or steering.

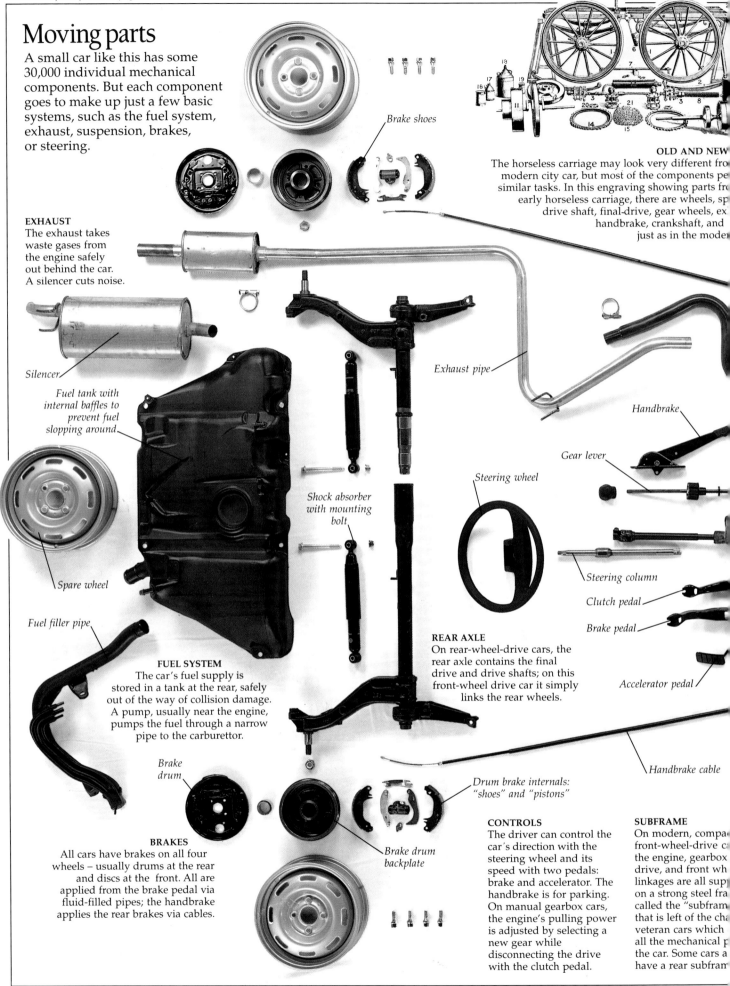

Brake shoes

OLD AND NEW
The horseless carriage may look very different fro modern city car, but most of the components pe similar tasks. In this engraving showing parts fro early horseless carriage, there are wheels, sp drive shaft, final-drive, gear wheels, ex handbrake, crankshaft, and just as in the mode

EXHAUST
The exhaust takes waste gases from the engine safely out behind the car. A silencer cuts noise.

Exhaust pipe

Silencer

Fuel tank with internal baffles to prevent fuel slopping around

Handbrake

Gear lever

Steering wheel

Shock absorber with mounting bolt

Steering column

Clutch pedal

Brake pedal

Spare wheel

Fuel filler pipe

FUEL SYSTEM
The car's fuel supply is stored in a tank at the rear, safely out of the way of collision damage. A pump, usually near the engine, pumps the fuel through a narrow pipe to the carburettor.

REAR AXLE
On rear-wheel-drive cars, the rear axle contains the final drive and drive shafts; on this front-wheel drive car it simply links the rear wheels.

Accelerator pedal

Handbrake cable

Brake drum

Drum brake internals: "shoes" and "pistons"

BRAKES
All cars have brakes on all four wheels – usually drums at the rear and discs at the front. All are applied from the brake pedal via fluid-filled pipes; the handbrake applies the rear brakes via cables.

Brake drum backplate

CONTROLS
The driver can control the car's direction with the steering wheel and its speed with two pedals: brake and accelerator. The handbrake is for parking. On manual gearbox cars, the engine's pulling power is adjusted by selecting a new gear while disconnecting the drive with the clutch pedal.

SUBFRAME
On modern, compa front-wheel-drive c the engine, gearbox drive, and front wh linkages are all sup on a strong steel fra called the "subfram that is left of the ch veteran cars which all the mechanical p the car. Some cars a have a rear subfram

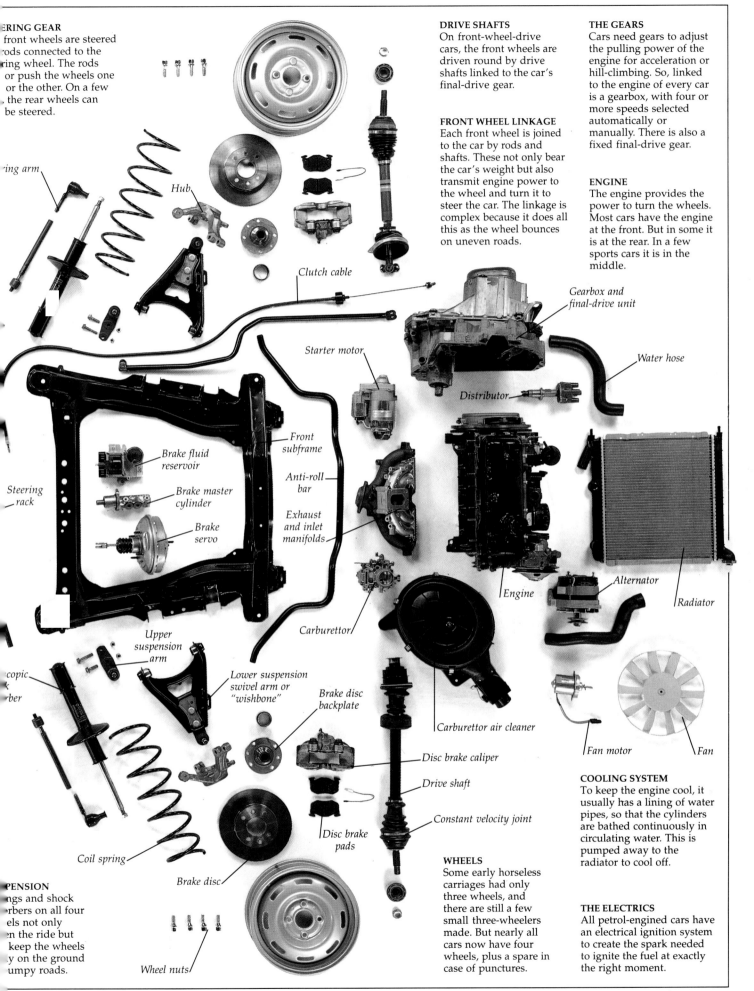

front wheels are steered
rods connected to the
ring wheel. The rods
or push the wheels one
or the other. On a few
, the rear wheels can
be steered.

ring arm

Hub

ring

DRIVE SHAFTS
On front-wheel-drive
cars, the front wheels are
driven round by drive
shafts linked to the car's
final-drive gear.

FRONT WHEEL LINKAGE
Each front wheel is joined
to the car by rods and
shafts. These not only bear
the car's weight but also
transmit engine power to
the wheel and turn it to
steer the car. The linkage is
complex because it does all
this as the wheel bounces
on uneven roads.

THE GEARS
Cars need gears to adjust
the pulling power of the
engine for acceleration or
hill-climbing. So, linked
to the engine of every car
is a gearbox, with four or
more speeds selected
automatically or
manually. There is also a
fixed final-drive gear.

ENGINE
The engine provides the
power to turn the wheels.
Most cars have the engine
at the front. But in some it
is at the rear. In a few
sports cars it is in the
middle.

Clutch cable

Starter motor

Gearbox and
final-drive unit

Water hose

Distributor

Front
subframe

Brake fluid
reservoir

Anti-roll
bar

Steering
rack

Brake master
cylinder

Exhaust
and inlet
manifolds

Brake
servo

Upper
suspension
arm

Carburettor

copic
k
rber

Lower suspension
swivel arm or
"wishbone"

Brake disc
backplate

Engine

Alternator

Radiator

Carburettor air cleaner

Fan motor

Fan

Disc brake caliper

Drive shaft

Disc brake
pads

Constant velocity joint

COOLING SYSTEM
To keep the engine cool, it
usually has a lining of water
pipes, so that the cylinders
are bathed continuously in
circulating water. This is
pumped away to the
radiator to cool off.

Coil spring

Brake disc

WHEELS
Some early horseless
carriages had only
three wheels, and
there are still a few
small three-wheelers
made. But nearly all
cars now have four
wheels, plus a spare in
case of punctures.

THE ELECTRICS
All petrol-engined cars have
an electrical ignition system
to create the spark needed
to ignite the fuel at exactly
the right moment.

PENSION
ngs and shock
rbers on all four
els not only
n the ride but
keep the wheels
y on the ground
umpy roads.

Wheel nuts

Continued on next page

The trim

While the car's mechanical and body parts make it go, it would not be a practical, usable machine without the trim: the seating, windows, tyres, electrical equipment, and decoration. Most trim items are attached to the car after the rest is fully assembled.

WHEEL TRIM
Hub caps are mostly for show, but also protect the wheel nuts and bearings from dirt and damp. Tyres may be "off-the-peg" or developed especially for the car.

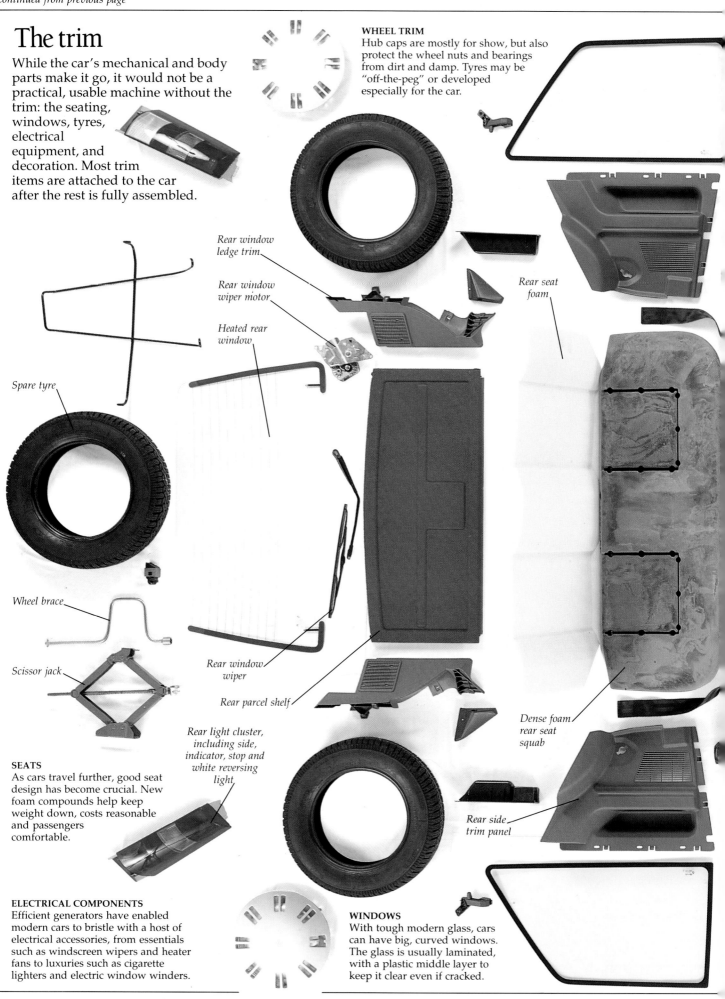

Rear window ledge trim

Rear window wiper motor

Heated rear window

Rear seat foam

Spare tyre

Wheel brace

Scissor jack

Rear window wiper

Rear parcel shelf

Dense foam rear seat squab

Rear light cluster, including side, indicator, stop and white reversing light

Rear side trim panel

SEATS
As cars travel further, good seat design has become crucial. New foam compounds help keep weight down, costs reasonable and passengers comfortable.

ELECTRICAL COMPONENTS
Efficient generators have enabled modern cars to bristle with a host of electrical accessories, from essentials such as windscreen wipers and heater fans to luxuries such as cigarette lighters and electric window winders.

WINDOWS
With tough modern glass, cars can have big, curved windows. The glass is usually laminated, with a plastic middle layer to keep it clear even if cracked.

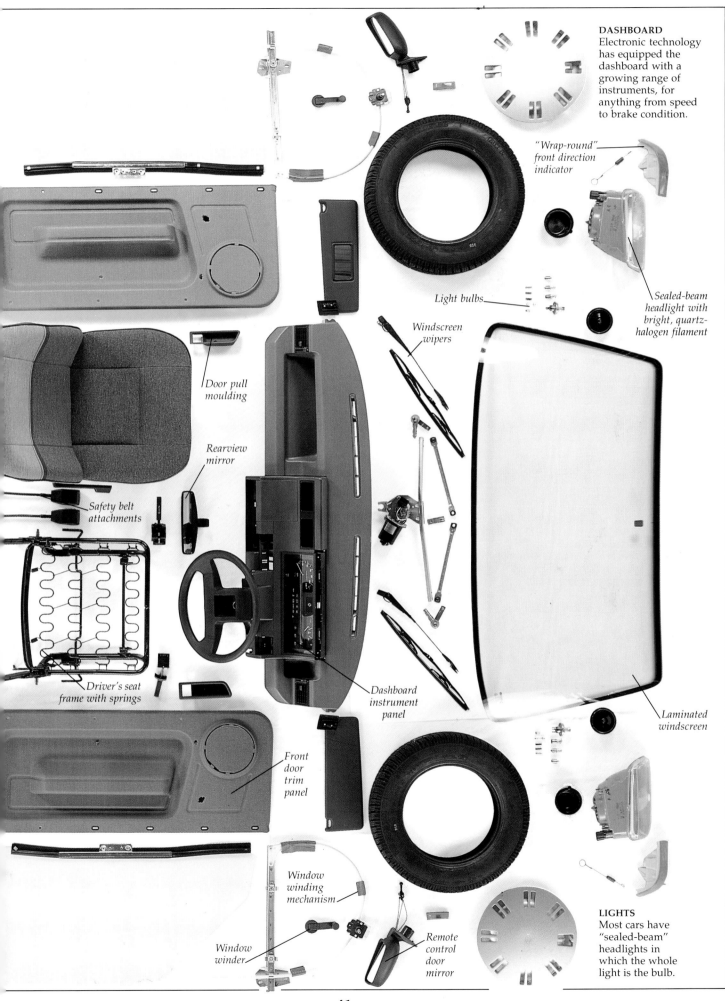

Electronic technology has equipped the dashboard with a growing range of instruments, for anything from speed to brake condition.

"Wrap-round" front direction indicator

Sealed-beam headlight with bright, quartz-halogen filament

Light bulbs

Windscreen wipers

Door pull moulding

Rearview mirror

Safety belt attachments

Laminated windscreen

Driver's seat frame with springs

Dashboard instrument panel

Front door trim panel

Window winding mechanism

Window winder

Remote control door mirror

LIGHTS
Most cars have "sealed-beam" headlights in which the whole light is the bulb.

The driving force

THE POWERHOUSE under the bonnet of nearly every modern car is an internal combustion engine – just as it was in the first Benz well over a century ago. Today's engines are powerful, compact, and economical compared to their forerunners. They usually have four or more small cylinders and run fast, too – unlike the massive single or twin cylinder engines of the early days which ticked over so slowly you could almost hear individual strokes of the piston. Yet the principles are still the same. The engine is a "combustion" engine because it "combusts" (burns) fuel, usually a mixture of petrol and air. It is an "internal" combustion engine because the fuel burns inside the cylinders.

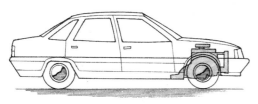

SMALL AND QUICK
Tucked away under the bonnet, modern car engines are compact, high revving, and powerful. This engine runs up to 6000 rpm (revolutions per minute) and its four 500 cc cylinders push out 40 times as much power as the Benz below.

SLOW AND SIMPLE
The single big 1140 cc cylinder of the 1898 Benz chugged around at a leisurely 1200 rpm. All the workings of the engine are clearly exposed here: the connecting rod running up inside the cylinder, the crankshaft, the big flywheel, and so on.

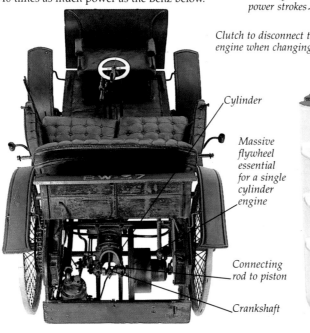

Cylinder

Massive flywheel essential for a single cylinder engine

Connecting rod to piston

Crankshaft

Distributor to send a spark to each cylinder at the right moment to start the fuel burning

Camshaft controls the opening and closing of the valves

Rocker to push valves

Channels for cooling water

Cylinders with perfectly smooth sides provide a channel for the pistons

Pistons slide up and down in the cylinders – and provide the driving force when pushed down by burning fuel

Flywheel of heavy steel to provide the momentum to carry the engine round smoothly between power strokes

Clutch to disconnect the engine when changing gear

Starter ring with teeth that mesh with teeth on the starter motor to spin the engine for starting

Crankshaft turns the up and down movement of the pistons into a "rotary" (spinning) movement

Piston and connecting rod turn the crank

EXPOSED ENGINE
The engine block and sump of this modern four-cylinder engine are cutaway to reveal the main mechanisms. For clarity, all the moving parts here are chrome-plated and the block is enamelled; in a complete engine, all the internals would be bare metal.

Strong springs to
snap valves shut

Combustion chamber –
where the fuel is burned
to force the piston down.

Valves let fresh fuel
into the combustion
chamber and spent
gases (exhaust) out

Separate airways
for fresh fuel and
exhaust

Thermostat
stops cooling
water
circulating
until the
engine is
running at
the right
temperature

Belt to drive the
water pump

Timing belt to
drive the
camshaft

Fan belt to
drive the
cooling fan

Dipstick for
checking oil level

"Sump" reservoir
for lubricating oil

nce weights act as
iterweights to the
ons and keep the
ne running smoothly

Crankshaft bearing
where the crankshaft
runs through the
engine block

BIG AND SMOOTH

The earliest car engines had only one or two cylinders;
most now have at least four because a four runs much
more smoothly. With one cylinder, there are big gaps
between "power strokes" (p. 44), making the engine
vibrate. With four, the power strokes on the other three
cylinders help fill in the gaps. In fact, the more cylinders
an engine has, the smoother it runs – this 5.3 litre Jaguar
engine has 12 cylinders and is very smooth indeed.

Engine layouts

The majority of modern car engines have four
pistons and cylinders set in line. Yet this is by
no means the only possible arrangement. Some
alternatives are shown below.

STRAIGHT SIX

Engines with six cylinders set in
line are very long, and costly to
make. But they can be very smooth
and powerful and are popular for
large, expensive saloons.

"V" SIX

Big straight engines are too long and
tall to fit into low-slung sports cars
and their long crankshafts can
"whip" under stress. So many sports
cars have compact "V" engines with
cylinders interlocking in a "V" and a
shorter, more rigid crankshaft.

FLAT FOUR

In cars such as the VW Beetle, the
cylinders are in two flat banks. The
engine is wide, but cool air can
reach the cylinders so easily that
water cooling is not always needed.

ROTARY ENGINE

Instead of pistons and cylinders, the
"Wankel" rotary engine has a pair
of three-cornered "rotors". These
rotate inside a chamber, drawing in
fuel, squeezing it until it is ignited,
then expelling the burned gases, in
one continuous movement. Rotary
engines are smooth and compact,
but expensive and often unreliable.

Rotor

Spark plugs

Inlet

Exhaust

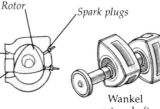

Wankel
rotor shaft

How the engine works

PETROL AND AIR is a dangerous mixture. Even the tiniest spark is enough to make it erupt into flame in an instant – which is why an engine works. Inside the cylinders, this deadly mixture is squeezed by the piston to make it even more ready to catch fire – and is then ignited by an electrical spark. It bursts into flame with almost explosive speed and expands so violently that it drives the piston back down the cylinder. It is this downward plunge of the piston – the "power stroke" – that spins the crankshaft and gives the engine its power. In nearly all car engines, this power stroke occurs once for every four times the piston goes up and down – which is, of course, why these engines are called "four-stroke" engines.

THE CAMSHAFT
Along each camshaft are lobes or "cams": one for e valve. As the cam rotates, each cam pushes its valve open in turn. Since the camshaft turns half as fas the crankshaft, each valve opens once for every two revolutions of the cranksh

Camshaft for inlet valves

Fuel meter to en that just the rig amount of fuel i injected into the cylinders (p. 49,

Exhaust "manifold" which channels waste gases and heat towards the exhaust pipe

Inlet valve

Fuel injector sprays petrol into the air streaming through the air intake

Air i

CROSS-SECTIONS
To show how the engine works, these two cross-sections (right and far right) were made by slicing across an engine as below. The engine is fairly advanced, with fuel-injection (p. 49) and double overhead camshafts – that is, it has two camshafts at the top of the engine above the cylinder head, one for the inlet valves and one for the exhaust

ABOUT TO FIRE
Here the piston is at the top of the cylinder, about to start its power stroke. Both valves are closed to seal in the mixture during combustion.

Waterways through which cooling water is pumped to carry heat away from the cylinders

HOT STUFF
The burning fuel releases hug amounts of energy. Barely a t of this energy can be used to drive the car; the rest is waste heat. Much of the heat goes straight out the exhaust; the r is carried away by the engine cooling system.

Generator

Section 1   Section 2

Balance weight

Oil temperature sensor

Oil filter

IN BALANCE
Notice how the crankshaft balance weights are directly below the piston when it is at the top of its stroke. This helps swing the piston down again for the next stroke.

SECTION ONE

LUBRICATION
To stop moving parts rubbing together, oil is pumped round the engine continuously to ke all moving parts separated by thin film of oil.

e four-stroke cycle

le the engine is running, every cyl-
r goes through the same sequence
ents, called the four-stroke cycle,
dreds of times a minute. The power
ke occurs in each cylinder only once
very two turns of the crankshaft.
he cylinders in a four-cylinder
ne fire one after another. So there is
ys a power stroke in one of them.

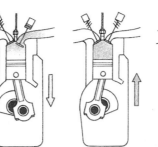

Induction:
piston
descending

Compression:
piston rising

Power: piston
descending

Exhaust:
piston
rising

THE CYCLE

The cycle begins with the
"induction" stroke. The inlet
valve opens and the piston slides
down the cylinder, sucking fuel
and air mixture (the "charge") in
behind. Then follows the "compression" stroke, when the valve
snaps shut, trapping the charge
in the cylinder, and the piston
rises, squeezing it into an ever
smaller space. When the piston is
nearly at the top, the spark flares
and the charge bursts into flame.
Expanding gases drive the piston back down for the "power"
stroke. Near the end of the
stroke, the exhaust valve opens.
Hot gases stream out, pushed by
the piston as it rises again. When
the piston reaches the top of
its "exhaust" stroke, the
cycle begins again.

E TIMING

, the engine is running at
rpm – that is, just ticking
– the valves open for barely
ntieth of a second each time.
s split second, the cylinder
fill with fuel and air, so the
must open and shut at
ely the right times – which
y the shape of each
s crucial.

*Camshaft for
exhaust valves*

*Electrical leads
to spark plugs*

Exhaust

Exhaust valve

COMPRESSION

ore the charge is squeezed by the rising
, the better it burns. So many high
rmance engines have a high "compression
to boost power – which means that the
s squeeze a lot of fuel into a tiny space.

*Specially shaped air intake
to ensure air flows into the
cylinders quickly*

Spark plug

*Piston rings ensure airtight
seal around the pistons*

Flywheel

*iston in lowest
osition, known as
'Bottom Dead Centre'*

T STROKE

cars, tall and narrow
ers meant the piston had
way to travel up and
– so the engine could only
owly. Modern cylinders
bbier and the piston's
e" much shorter – so the
e can run much faster.

Big end bearing

*Oil channel
through
crankshaft*

Crankshaft

SECTION TWO

POWER BLOCKS

Car engines vary
in size and look,
but nearly all depend on the four-stroke cycle.
Nevertheless, in the 30 years that separate the
six-litre Ford V8 of the late 1950s (above)
from the competition Renault V10 (below),
engines have improved considerably both in
power and economy – through the use of
new, lighter materials, improved fuel supply
and ignition, and better valve gear.

Inside the engine

Take an engine apart and you will find that it is really quite simple inside. You will see the drum-shaped pistons that ride up and down, pushing and pulling on steel connecting rods to turn the crankshaft. You will see the crankshaft itself, the strong zig-zag rod that drives the car's wheels as it turns. You will see the trumpet-like valves that let fuel into the cylinders and the exhaust gases out. And you will see the solid engine block and cylinder head that hold it all in place. But though the parts are simple, they must be immensely tough to withstand the heat and stress. Temperatures reach a ferocious 1700°C (3000°F) inside the cylinders, and the pistons have to bear pressures of up to 15 tonnes. They must be accurately made, too, for the engine to run smoothly and well.

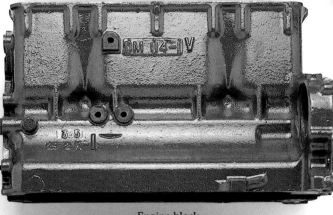

Ai
Carbu

Spark plugs
and leads

Petrol pump

BLOCK HEAD
The cylinder head is basically a big block of metal that seals the top of the cylinders. There are slots for the valves bored through it and tunnels to carry fuel and exhaust to and from the cylinders. Little dishes, cut into the underside, form the combustion chambers (p. 42).

(p. 42)

Oil filler

OLD FAVOURITE
Until front-wheel drive cars became popular in the 1980s, most engines and their external components looked much like this.

Ger

Inlet ports (2)   Rocker cover   Exhaust ports (4)

Cylinder head

Water
pump

Inlet
manifold to
pipe new
fuel to the
cylinders

Manifolds

Exhaust
manifold to carry
waste gases away

PIPEWORK
The "manifolds" are the branching metal pipes that carry the fuel and air mixture into the engine and the exhaust gases away.

DM 114-1V

Engine block

BORED RIGID
The engine block is strong and heavy; i to be, for the cylind are bored through i the block has to sta to tremendous heat pressure. Bored thr the block are also h for cooling water a to circulate, and, in engines, for the val pushrods.

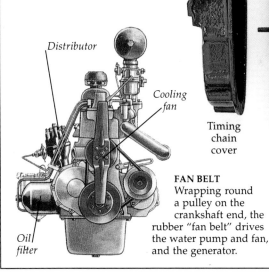

Distributor

Cooling
fan

Oil
filter

Timing
chain
cover

FAN BELT
Wrapping round a pulley on the crankshaft end, the rubber "fan belt" drives the water pump and fan, and the generator.

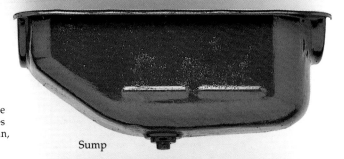

Sump

OIL BATH
After a few thousand m driving, the oil in the su gets thin and black with It must be changed for f oil if it is to lubricate the engine properly.

...CING BACK
...ach valve
...g up to 50 times
...nd, the springs
...ap them shut
...e really strong
...trong that
...t the little inner
...the valve might
...e open again.

...AND SHUT CASE
...simplest engines,
...re two valves for
...ylinder, an inlet
...and a slightly
...r exhaust.

Piston and
gudgeon pin

Connecting
rod and
gudgeon pin

...TON AND ROD
...iston and conrod
...up and down the
...er up to 6000 times
...ute, and travel at
...s of 500 kmh (300
...ph) or more.

Exhaust valve   Inlet valve

Grooves for
piston rings

Gudgeon pin

Piston

Little end

Connecting
rod

Big end

LINKING UP
By encircling the crankpin at the
bottom or "big end" and the
gudgeon pin at the top or "little
end", the connecting rod links
the crankshaft.

VALVE TRAIN
In older engines, the
camshaft is at the
bottom of the engine
near the crank, and
the valves are
operated through a
series of rods called
"pushrods".

Rocker
arm

SEALING RINGS
To prevent gases leaking
from the cylinder past the
pistons, each piston has a
series of sealing rings.

ROCKERS
Pushrods open the
valves via rocker
arms.

...nd for
...ulley to
...ater
...nd
...or,

...kshaft
...l" which
...the main
...g in the
...e block

Flywheel

Crankpin which
carries the big end of
the connecting rod

Balance weight or "web"

BIT OF A CRANK
Forged as a single piece, the crankshaft must be perfectly
balanced to avoid vibration. The smooth crankpins, where
the shaft is encircled by the big end and main bearings,
must be machined to an accuracy of 0.01 mm.

Starter ring

Fuel and air

B$_Y$ A HAPPY COINCIDENCE, petrol was discovered in 1857 – just two years before Étienne Lenoir built the first internal combustion engine (p. 6). Most car engines have run on petrol ever since. Although other fuels will work – cars have even run on the methane gas given off by manure – petrol has proved by far the most practical. However, no engine runs well if the petrol is not fed in as a very fine spray, mixed with air in precisely the right proportion. A fuel mixture over-rich in petrol burns like a damp squib, and petrol is wasted. A "lean" mixture, on the other hand, contains so little petrol that all of it is burned up far too soon to give a powerful push on the piston. So since the days of the pioneers, most cars have had some form of "carburettor" to feed the engine with the right fuel mixture. Carburettors work reasonably well and are cheap to make. But, for a more accurately metered fuel supply, many sportier cars now have "fuel injectors" instead.

Air flows in here (sometimes called the "choke")

"Throttle" rotates to restrict air flow and control engine speed

Float sin... opens n... valve wh... the fuel drop...

Neck or "venturi"

Jet

Mixture to engine

Needle v... controllin... supply fr... the pump

JET PROPELLED *above*
This early carburettor, cut in half to show the inside, looks very different from those of today (right). Yet it works in much the same way. Like drink through a straw, petrol is sucked from a little reservoir called the float chamber by air streaming through the neck of the carburettor. It emerges in a fine spray through a thin tube or "jet" and flows with the air into the engine.

Fuel out

Pump p...

Fuel in

Sludge trap

Pum... wor... and d... the cra...

PETROL SHOP *above*
In the early days, petrol had to be bought in 2-gallon (10-litre) cans and poured into the tank through a funnel.

FILL IT UP, PLEASE
Cans soon gave way to pumps that drew petrol up from an underground tank. The first were hand-operated and delivered fuel in fixed amounts from a glass dispenser. By the 1920s (below), filling stations had mechanical pumps with flow meters.

BACK TO FRONT *right*
A pump draws petrol from the car's tank to fill the carburettor float chamber.

LEAD POWER *right*
In the 1920s, tinkering with the carb was one way of improving performance. Far better, though, was to add lead to the petrol, first tried in 1923. The more the fuel charge is compressed, the better the engine performs (p. 45). But too much makes the charge "detonate" or explode violently rather than burn smoothly, damaging the engine. Lead in petrol allowed high compression without detonation and so better performance. So well did it work that for 60 years, nearly all cars ran on petrol with lead added in varying proportions or "octane ratings". Only recently did unleaded petrol come back as people realized how bad lead was for health.

[VARI]ABLE JET

[In thi]s carburettor, a neat system
[ensur]es the fuel-air mixture is right,
[no ma]tter how fast the engine is
[runni]ng. A tapered needle controls
[how m]uch fuel sprays from the jet
[and a] piston controls how much air
[flows] through the neck of the
[carbu]rettor. Since they both
[move] up and down together,
[the m]ixture stays constant.

*Damper to stop
piston fluttering
up and down*

Piston

*Tapered
needle*

[Flo]at chamber

Jet

Float

Jet adjuster

[DOUB]LE BARREL

[Some] high performance cars
[have] carburettors with two
[barr]es", like this
[one,] Weber. With
[two ch]okes, fuel
[can fl]ow that much
[faster] into the
[engin]e – especially
[when i]t is as broad
[ly o]pen as
[they] are.

Choke

[FUEL I]NJECTION

[Carbu]rettors rely on the
[engin]e to suck in as much
[petrol] it needs; fuel
[injecto]rs deliver exactly
[what t]he engine should
[need. T]he injectors are
[like sy]ringes that squirt
[petrol] into the air intake
[to each] cylinder. A
[sophist]icated metering
[system] ensures that each
[cylinder i]s just right.

Turbo power

Turbochargers first showed
their real potential on racing
cars in 1978; now they are used
on many high performance
road cars to boost power. Like
superchargers, they work by
squeezing extra charge into
cylinders.

SELF-PROPELLED

Unlike superchargers, which are belt-
driven, the rotor vanes of a turbo are
spun by the exhaust as it rushes from
the cylinders. As the vanes spin they
turn another rotor in the inlet which
forces in the extra
charge.

*Exhaust
in*

*Exhaust
out*

Inlet rotor

Exhaust rotor

SPECIAL VANES

Because the turbo's vanes
spin round extremely fast
and get very hot, they have
to be carefully engineered.

HORN BLOWER

The turbo's inlet
duct broadens
out like a horn
to build up the
air pressure.

Inlet duct

Inlet rotor

*Cable from
accelerator pedal
pulls here to
open throttle
flaps*

Jet

*Throttle
flap*

Choke

THE THROTTLE

Feed a lot of fuel
into the engine and it runs fast;
feed in a little and it runs slow. So the accelerator pedal controls the car's
speed by varying how much fuel is fed to the engine. With carburettors,
the pedal turns a flap called the "throttle" which opens and shuts to vary
the flow of air (and fuel) through the carburettor.

The vital spark

THE SPARK PLUG MAY BE SMALL, but it is vital. It is the spark plug that ignites the charge to send the piston shooting down the cylinder. It is actually just part of a powerful electrical circuit, and the twin points of the plug, the "electro are simply a gap in the circuit. Ten, 25, even 50 times a second, the c is switched on, and the current sizzles across the gap like a flash of lightning to ignite the charge. It needs a huge current – at least 14,0 volts – for the spark to leap the gap. Yet the car's battery only give volts. So the current is run through a coil, with thousands of winding copper wire, to boost it dramatically for an instant. The massive current then sent off to the right cylinder by the "distributor". For the engine to well, it must spark in the cylinder at exactly the right time. A spark that comes too early catches the fuel charge before it is completely compressed by the rising piston – so it burns unevenly. A spark that comes too late wastes some of the power of the charge. Some cars still have the traditional "points" to time the spark; most now have electronic "pointless" systems.

Plugs may have changed . . .

HEAVING IT INTO LIFE
Before the days of electric starters, motorists had to start their cars by hand. A mighty swing or two on the starting handle was hopefully enough to send the engine spluttering into life. But strained muscles were all too common.

BUTTON START *left*
The electric starter motor – first seen on a Cadillac in 1911 – was seen as a great boon for lady drivers.

KEY START *right*
Carmakers soon added a key switch to the electric starter button – when drivers realized that anyone could jump into the car and drive off!

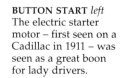

OLD SPARK
Up until the 1930s, most cars "magneto" rather than a provide the ignition v The magneto was a n that spun betwee coils to gen huge current. the contr

CAR ELECTRICS *right*
A car would not run without a good electrical system. It needs electricity to turn the engine for starting, to fire the ignition, and to power the lights, windscreen wipers and other accessories. Electrical systems have become much more complicated over the years but still retain the same basic elements as in this 1930s diagram.

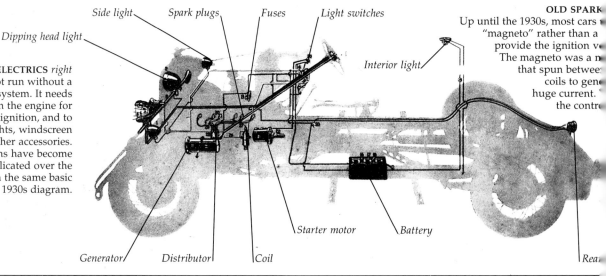

Side light — Spark plugs — Fuses — Light switches

Dipping head light

Interior light

Generator — Distributor — Coil — Starter motor — Battery — Rea

...TION CIRCUIT

...are the
...ponents of coil
...ion laid out. The
...am is for an early
...ut the principles
...in the same. The
...ibutor base acts
...a switch for the
..."tension" (LT; low
...age) circuit which
...ects the battery to
...oil's outer
...ings. When the
...ibutor switches
...e LT circuit, a
...voltage is
...rated in the coil's
...windings. This
...s through the
...ibutor cap to the
...spark plug.

Distributor cap

Distributor base

Low tension circuit

Spark plug

High tension circuit

Coil

Ignition switch

Battery

"Earth" connection to car body

HOT TIPS *right and below*
Spark plugs look
simple yet they
have to withstand
enormous
temperatures and
still work well,
so plug design
has changed
considerably
over the years.

Core

Electrode

Inside old spark plugs,
revealing the core and
central electrode

. . . a great deal over the years . . .   . . . but they still do . . .   . . . much the same job.

...ING THE SPARK

...der distributors (below), the LT circuit
...tched off and on by a mechanical
...act breaker" or "points" opened and
...by the distributor shaft as it rotates.
...most work electronically (right),
...n makes them more reliable.

*Vacuum advance
provides earlier spark
at high speeds*

*...g "rotor arm"
...he HT circuit
...e right spark
...lug lead*

*Condenser
strengthens
the spark*

*Points open to
break the LT
circuit and
create a spark*

*Distributor
shaft driven by the
engine operates the
points and turns
the rotor arm.*

*High tension
lead connector*

*Low tension
circuit
connectors*

*Early
ignition
coil*

UPPING THE VOLTS
The "coil" is actually two coils,
wrapped round a magnetic core.
The outer, LT coil has a few
hundred turns of thick wire; the
inner, HT coil has thousands of
turns of thin wire – up to 1.6 km
(1 mile) long in all.

Cell terminals

*Individual
battery
cells*

POWER STORE
Modern car batteries can store
a great deal of power – enough to
power the sidelights for almost a week.
But all the car's electrical power comes from
the battery; it would soon run down if not
continuously recharged by the generator.

*Early
car battery*

The drive train

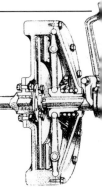

IN THE VERY FIRST CARS, the engine was linked more or less directly to the driving wheels. Nowadays, the engine turns the wheels through a series of shafts and gears called the "transmission" or "drive", and every car has a gearbox. Cars need gearboxes because engines work well only when running at certain speeds. With no gearbox, the car too could only go at certain speeds. It could start off briskly perhaps, or cruise swiftly along the motorway – but not both. What the gearbox does is change how fast the wheels turn relative to the engine. To drive the wheels faster or slower, the driver selects a different gear – while the engine stays running in the same speed range. But it is not just a question of speed. Extra effort is needed to get the car moving, to accelerate, and to drive uphill. The slower ("high ratio") gears provide this extra effort by concentrating more of the engine's power into each turn of the wheel. The faster gears are for economical high-speed cruising.

THE CLUTCH
The engine's flywheel dr the gearbox via the dis shaped "clutch plate". T clutch plate and flywheel usually pressed firmly together and rotate as o

ENGINE AND GEARBOX
The gearbox is bolted straight on to the end of the engine, with the clutch in between. During gear changes, the driver presses the clutch pedal to pull the clutch plate back from the flywheel and temporarily disconnect the engine.

"Universal" joints allow the shaft to hinge up and down

Clutch

Transm t

Gearbox

Propeller shaft

Fina

CHAINED UP
Many early cars had a chain drive, just like a bicycle chain. It was simple but effective, and flexed easily up and down as the carriage bounced along.

REAR WHEEL DRIVE
Until recently, nearly all cars were driven by the rear wheels, and the transmission ran back from the engine right under the length of the car.

REAR ENGINE
With the engine at the back, the famous Volkswagen Beetle's gearbox is at the back, too, between the rear wheels. The car had no rear axle. Instead the wheels were driven by short drive shafts which emerged at right angles from the gearbox.

Gearbo.

Gear change lever

ears

ars are pairs of wheels with
h that interlock so that as one
s it drives the other round
h it. If the gears are the same
, they both turn at the same
ed. But if one gear is smaller,
bigger gear turns slower yet
more force. Just how much
ver and more forcefully
ends on the gear
io" – that is, the
erence in size.

T A MESH!

ging gear in early cars was a real
The driver had to get the engine
d just right for the spinning gear
to mesh without crunching. Now,
e gear pairs are constantly meshed
her. On one shaft, the gears are fixed
turn with it, but on the other they
loosely. When a gear is
ed, the right loose gear is
d to its shaft by a
g collar that meshes
teeth called "dogs"
e side of the gear.

Dogs

Gear

Output shaft

Baulk ring to help match the speed of the gear and the collar before they interlock

R PATHS

cars have four or
forward gears –
one reverse – and
ear pairs are often
ong an "input"
an "output" shaft.
e the engine is
ing, the input shaft
gears turn all the
and the output
turn with them. But
a gear is engaged,
utput shaft stays
Once a gear is
ged, the chosen
ut gear is locked to
haft, and so turns
haft with it.
while, the other
ut gears continue to
loosely.

Top gear

Input shaft

Reverse gear

Baulk ring

Locking collar

Splines to secure locking collar to shaft

Bottom gear

THE GEARBOX *right and below*
This a typical gearbox from a modern front-wheel-drive car. It is a "manual" box – which means that the driver makes all the gear changes. With "automatic" boxes, the changes are made automatically when the engine reaches certain speeds.

Neutral (no gear engaged)

1st or bottom

2nd

3rd

Input

Output

4th or top

Reverse

Half shaft

Final-drive unit and differential

GEARED UP
The biggest gear on the gearbox output shaft meshes with the smallest on the input shaft. This is "first" or "bottom" gear, and it turns the wheels slowly but strongly for starting off. The "top" gear cogs on each shaft are the same size, turning the wheels quickly but weakly, for cruising at speed.

GOING BACKWARDS
In reverse, the drive goes through a third shaft that turns the output the other way.

Final-drive gear

FINAL-DRIVE GEAR
The largest gear is the last: the final-drive gear. In front-wheel-drive cars, this is a single big cog in the gearbox (right). With rear-wheel-drive, however, it is in the middle of the back axle (left) and is linked to a set of gears called the "differential". These gears ensure that when the car goes round a bend, the wheel on the inside of the bend – which travels a shorter distance than the outer wheel – rotates slower.

Smoothing the ride

Cars were first given springs to cushion passengers from bumps and jolts; with the solid tyres and rutted roads of the early days, they really needed them. Pneumatic tyres and tarred roads have since made life much more comfortable. Even so, travelling by car would still be painful without springs to soften the ride. Yet springs are far more than just cushions. A car's suspension – its springs and dampers – is fundamental to the way it stops, starts, and goes round corners. Without it, the car would leap around dangerously all over the road – which is why modern suspension is so carefully designed.

Leaf springs

Fitted to horse carts long before cars were invented, leaf springs are the oldest form of car suspension. They are made from curved strips or "leaves" of steel, bound together by metal bands. They bend whenever the car hits a bump, but soon spring back to their original shape.

BW-37

Leaf spring for each wh[eel]

CART TO CAR
On horse carts, only the body was carried on the springs; on cars, the chassis and engine was too – otherwise it would all have shaken to bits very quickly.

Rear axle usually clamped here with U-shaped bolts

Eye for fixing spring to the main structure of the car

Metal band to hold leaves together

More leaves for extra strength in centre

Semi-e[lliptic] (fro[nt]

Semi-elliptic (rear)

Three-quarter elliptic

LEAF FORMS
Most leaf springs were bow-shaped or "semi-elliptical" but there were many other types in the early days. Cantilevers, with the axle attached to the end of the spring rather than the middle, were popular for luxury cars.

Cantilever

CROSS-SPRING
The 1908 Ford Model T's suspension was quite unusual at the time. Most cars then had four springs running lengthways, one for each wheel. The cost-conscious Model T (pp. 16–17) had just two, running across the car at front and back. It tended to roll and sway, but worked – even in the 1960s, some sports cars had very similar systems.

Front suspension consisting of single leaf spring which bends upwards whenever the car rides over a bump

Single central mounting point for spring makes the car prone to roll and sway

SPRINGS AND SHOCKERS
Dampers are often wrongly called shock absorbers. But it is the springs that "absorb the shock" as the car hits a bump; the dampers damp down the springing and stop the springs bouncing the wheels long afterwards. Ideally, the wheels would follow the bumps exactly, while the car stayed perfectly level.

oil springs

st cars now use small and light
springs which can cope better
a much bigger range of
ps than leaf springs. They
d firm mounting at either end
ey are not to wobble from side
de. But they combine neatly
effectively with telescopic
pers in a single unit.

*Coil
spring*

*Damper
piston
arm*

OTH,
LE AND SAFE...
id the brochure for the 1950s
ber saloon shown here. Large
prings were held firmly in place
e front between two triangular
or "wishbones".

PENDENT SPRINGS
nally, front wheels were
d by a rigid axle, and the
t of any bump was sent
wheel to wheel. Inde-
ent front suspension
t the wheels were
ted and each had its
separate suspension.
y cars now have
pendent rear
ension as well,
his Lotus.

*Fluid-filled
damper body,
which slides
up round
damper piston*

SPRING MATCH *above*
Telescopic hydraulic
dampers slot neatly
inside coil springs – an
arrangement used on
most cars nowadays.

Fluid springs

Most cars still have basic
metal springs. But over the
years, ingenious hydraulic
(fluid-based) systems have
been used. Some racing cars
now have "active" systems
that use a computer to
adjust the suspension to suit
the road surface.

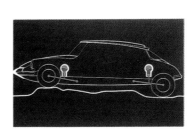

SELF-LEVELLING *left and above*
Citroen's "hydrogas" system
combines a fluid-filled damper
(red above) with a gas "cushion"
(blue). With any change in weight,
fluid is automatically pumped into
the damper or let out – keeping
the car level all the time.

Dampers

Dampers are a vital brake on the
springs – in the days before
dampers, a Vauxhall once bounced
clean over a hedge after hitting a
bump. The first dampers relied on
friction. Now most are hydraulic
and the spring is slowed by
forcing fluid through tiny holes.

*Double
tube and
piston*

*Twisting
disc*

OLD DAMPERS *above*
Until 1940, most
dampers relied on the
friction between two
rubbing surfaces to
slow the springs
down.

ROUGH RIDING *above*
Friction dampers were
mounted between the
leaf spring and the
chassis, or with double
springs, across the gap
(see inset).

*"Wishbone"
forming lower
suspension
linkage*

Drive shaft

SHARED LOAD
On this Lotus, light tube
"wishbones" combine with
the drive shafts to form the
rear suspension linkage.

Stopping and steering

A DRIVER HAS TWO MAIN WAYS of controlling the car on the move – by braking and by steering. Both controls work through the wheels. The main braking system – activated by the brake pedal – slows all four wheels simultaneously. An additional, hand-operated, brake locks either the front or back wheels to stop the car running away when parked on hills. To steer, the front wheels alone are turned, although a few cars can now be steered with all four wheels. But when either braking or steering (or both) the tyres must always be in firm contact with the road. If the road is slippery – perhaps due to rain or ice – the tyres can slide across the surface, so that the driver can neither stop nor steer properly. Similarly, the car can skid out of control if the driver brakes or turns so hard that the tyres lose their grip on the road.

ON THE RACK
Most cars today rely on a steering mechanism called a "rack and pinion" – a special gear (p. 53) that makes it easier to turn the wheels. The pinion is simply the splined end of the steering column; the rack is a row of teeth on a rod linked to the wheels at either end. When the driver turns the steering wheel, the pinion rolls the rack along, so the rack pulls on one wheel and pushes on the other.

HELP! HELP!
Brakes were never very effective in the early days – and often failed altogether. Weaker drivers could not hope to pull on the brake lever hard enough to bring a speeding car to a halt.

End of steering shaft from wheel

Link to wheel

Track rod

Rubber protective gaiter

Swivelling "ball joint"

Honda four-wheel steering system

Pinion

Rack

Rack cut ... half here f... illustratio...

Old-fashioned steering arrangement

ON ALL FOURS *left*
Four-wheel steering makes parking much easier and gives better control at speed. At high speed, the back wheels turn in the same direction as the front, but at low speeds they turn the opposite way.

THE WORM TURNS *right*
Many early cars had "worm and nut" steering systems. The worm is the end of the steering column, cut with a spiral thread. As it turns, the thread moves the sleeve-like nut to and fro.

FROM WHEEL TO W...
Between the steering whee... the road wheels, the ste... system on every car has muc... same basic elements: a ste... column containing the ... turned by the steering wh... steering gearbox to make it ... to turn the wheels and to co... the turning of the shaft into a ... fro motion; and a system o... and levers to swivel the w... one way or the ...

Hydraulic brakes

Applying the brakes hard enough to stop a heavy, fast moving car demands considerable force. So the brakes on every car are operated "hydraulically". This means that when the driver presses the brake pedal, a piston forces fluid down pipes from a "master cylinder" to pistons that apply the brakes on each of the wheels. Because the pistons at the wheels are much bigger than the piston in the master cylinder, the effect is to multiply the force applied to the brakes.

Steering wheel

Brake disc

Large area of metal for rapid cooling

Brake disc "caliper" housing pistons and pads

Brake on

Brake off

STOP GAP
The pads are squeezed on to the disc by hydraulic pressure.

DISC BRAKES
Powerful and efficient disc brakes are used on the front wheels of most modern cars. They work by squeezing a pair of pads on to a metal disc attached to the inside of the wheel. Just like bicycle brake pads, the pads rub on the disc and slow it down, slowing the wheel in the process.

Steering column and gearbox c 1910

Steering column containing steering shaft

Brake shoe

Brake drum (cutaway)

Hydraulic cylinder housing piston

OLD SHOES
The arrangement of shoes in the drum has changed little since the early days when brakes were operated by rods.

DRUM BRAKES
Old-fashioned drum brakes are usually adequate for the rear wheels, and work well as parking brakes. Each drum brake has two curved pads or "shoes" that sit inside a metal drum that spins with the wheel. When the brake is applied, the shoes are pushed outwards and rub against the inside of the drum, slowing it down.

Brake pad

Short worm gear

Steering gearbox

Changing wheels

A CAR WHEEL has a demanding role to play. It needs a good airtight rim to hold the tyre in place. It must be strong, too, to bear the car's weight. And it has to be tough to stand up t the forces of braking, acceleration, and road bumps. Above all, though, a car wheel has to be as light as possible, for easy starting and stopping, and to keep the car's "unsprung weight" (p. 55) to a minimum. To meet these demands, wheels have evolved steadily since the pioneering days when wheels were big simply to give the car sufficient clearance over rutted roads. The first car wheels were adapted from horse carts and were very heavy. Or they cam from bicycles and were weak. The car wheels of today are made from pressed-steel or light alloys and are small, light, and strong.

HURRY, THERE, JAMES!
Carrying a spare wheel in case of punctures was still such a new idea in 1912 that it was a major selling point for wheel and tyre manufacturers like Dunlop.

Detachable wooden rim pieces or "felloes"

Cast-iron hub

Iron binding

Hollov pre

Splined hub for quick wheel change

RIGHT WHEEL
Cartwheel origins are unmistakable in this World War I lorry wheel. The spokes are cast-iron, but the rim is wooden. The wheel is immensely heavy, but strong enough to carry heavy guns. Wheels like this, and the bolt-on wheel to the right, were called "artillery" wheels.

Bolt-on hub for quick wheel change

BOLT-ON, BOLT-OFF
Punctures were common in the early days, so the launch of the Sankey wheel 1910 was a godsend for drivers. It could be unbolted and replaced with a spare in minut Made of pressed-steel, it was also strong and compared to wooden wheels.

Fit hub mou

WIRED UP
For many years, cars used either Sankey-type steel wheels or wire wheels descended from the bicycle. Early wire wheels were very light and the spokes absorbed some road shocks. But the simple radial pattern of spokes meant they were not very strong. On larger wheels the spokes would bend and "whip" at speed.

Simple radial spokes prone to "whip"

Treadless tyre for minimum resistance

BIG WHEEL above and ri
This tyre fitted one of the wheels of Malcolm Camp
land speed record break
"Bluebird" of 1935 (see i right). Such big wheels gav car tremendous speed ove ground before the engi reached its rev limit.

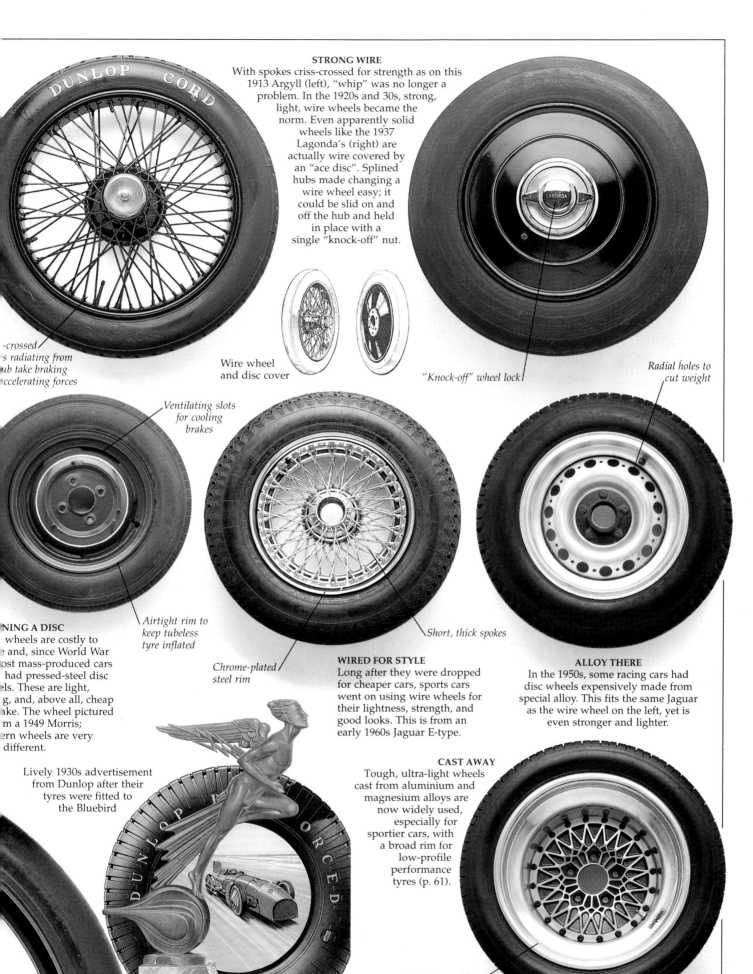

STRONG WIRE

With spokes criss-crossed for strength as on this 1913 Argyll (left), "whip" was no longer a problem. In the 1920s and 30s, strong, light, wire wheels became the norm. Even apparently solid wheels like the 1937 Lagonda's (right) are actually wire covered by an "ace disc". Splined hubs made changing a wire wheel easy; it could be slid on and off the hub and held in place with a single "knock-off" nut.

-crossed
s radiating from
ub take braking
ccelerating forces

Wire wheel
and disc cover

"Knock-off" wheel lock

Radial holes to
cut weight

Ventilating slots
for cooling
brakes

NING A DISC

wheels are costly to
e and, since World War
ost mass-produced cars
had pressed-steel disc
ls. These are light,
g, and, above all, cheap
ake. The wheel pictured
m a 1949 Morris;
ern wheels are very
different.

Lively 1930s advertisement
from Dunlop after their
tyres were fitted to
the Bluebird

Airtight rim to
keep tubeless
tyre inflated

Chrome-plated
steel rim

Short, thick spokes

WIRED FOR STYLE

Long after they were dropped for cheaper cars, sports cars went on using wire wheels for their lightness, strength, and good looks. This is from an early 1960s Jaguar E-type.

ALLOY THERE

In the 1950s, some racing cars had disc wheels expensively made from special alloy. This fits the same Jaguar as the wire wheel on the left, yet is even stronger and lighter.

CAST AWAY

Tough, ultra-light wheels cast from aluminium and magnesium alloys are now widely used, especially for sportier cars, with a broad rim for low-profile performance tyres (p. 61).

Split-rim enables
just outer rim to be
replaced if damaged

Riding on air

GOOD TYRES ARE VITAL for safety and performance. Unless the tyres "grip securely on many road surfaces – in the wet, in the dry, on rough roads, an on smooth – the car can not stop, corner, or even accelerate effectively. Tyres must also give a comfortable ride, run easily, and wear well. They have improved dramatically over the years and modern "pneumatic" (air-filled) tyres usually do this well, as long as they are in good condition. Careful des of the strengthening cords and webbing keeps the tyre the right shape, no matter how it is squashed or pulled. The tread (the pattern of grooves) push water out of the way and keeps the tyre in contact with the road.

MICHELIN MAN
One of the oldest tyre manufacturers of all is the French Michelin company. "Bibendum", the Michelin Man made out of Michelin tyres, is their famous trademark.

ANOTHER FLAT!
A puncture once meant a roadside repair.

BRUTE FORCE
There was no spare wheel, so the tyre had to be levered forcefully off the wheel rim, and the inner tube repaired.

TYRE AID
Once cars carried a spare wheel, the wheel could be swapped and the puncture repaired later by a professional.

Rubber knobs to stop the wheel sliding and spinning on mud roads

Bumps to improve traction a little

Grooves angled in direction of rotation to aid grip on hills

Primitive tread pattern

Long chann water flow quick from under the r of th

SOLID RUBBER c 1915
The first tyres were solid rubber. They gave a hard ride, but never punctured and were used on lorries long after cars went pneumatic.

CUSHION TYRE c 1903
Long used on bicycles, pneumatic tyres were first fitted to a car in 1895. They gave a much softer ride and soon replaced solid tyres.

EARLY TREAD c 1906
Smooth early tyres skidded wildly on damp roads. So drivers tried leather wheel covers and different tread patterns.

DUNLOP c 1909
Early pneumatic tyres had an inner tube and were narrow. They were also pumped up to high pressure to help keep them on the rim.

BALLOON TYRE
By 1930, cars we using wider "balloon" tyres ran at much low pressure than ea tyres and gave a softer, smoother

60

LITTLE FOOTPRINT
Only a tiny area of the tyre touches the road so tread design is crucial.

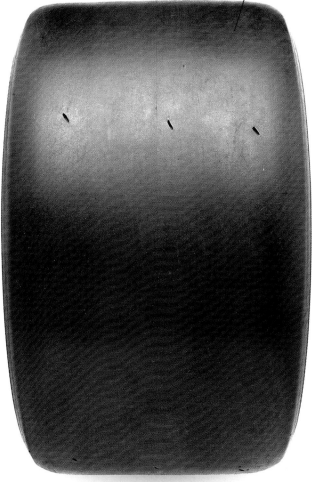

RE-TYRING
When early tyres punctured, motorists repaired them "vulcanizing" with a sulphur mixture.

TREADING CAREFULLY
A tyre's tread provides channels for water to flow out quickly and safely from under the tyre, where it might otherwise reduce grip. It also gives plenty of edges for extra "bite" on the road.

WEBS AND CORDS
Rubber tyres are reinforced by a network of nylon, rayon or steel cords and webbing.

THE TYRE FOR THE JOB
Racing cars use the right tyre for the conditions – treadless "slicks" for dry tracks, tyres with different treads for wet. Tyres for road cars are a compromise to suit all kinds conditions.

channels
water
edges
quickly
side

Little incisions in the tyre mop up water like a sponge

Water can accumulate in small ponds before it drains away

Tyres have become wider and more squat ("low profile") to increase the area of tyre in contact with the road for good grip

Slicks get extra grip as the rubber compound gets hot and sticky during the race

TUBELESS TYRE c 1947
In the post-war years, strong, broad, air-tight wheel rims made an inner tube unnecessary. Now, low-pressure, "tubeless" tyres are almost universal.

RADIAL-PLY c 1972
In earlier tyres, strengthening cords ran diagonally across the tyre ("cross-ply"). Now most cars use "radial-ply" tyres with cords running radially out from the wheel's centre.

RACING SLICK
In dry weather, modern racing cars use huge smooth tyres called "slicks" to put as much rubber as possible in touch with the track for good grip.

Marques and makes

IN THE EARLY DAYS, HUNDREDS OF COMPANIES, large and small, made cars. In 1913, there were 200-odd different car "marques" (makers' names) in the USA alone. Each marque had its own mascot, badge or label, to distinguish its cars from the rest. These emblems were status symbols, and were often beautifully made from hand-painted enamel, or even precious metals. But as mass-production made cars cheaper, more and more of the smaller companies were swallowed up by the giants, or driven out of business altogether. Many of the badges shown here are a poignant reminder of marques long since vanished – forgotten names such as Chalmers, Bean, Swift, and Stutz. Cars still have badges today, but they are generally much plainer.

DRAGO
Mascots became so popu
the 1920s that many ov
had them specially made
exquisite glass ra
mascots of the F
sculptor René La
were famous
dragonfly, like
"Laliques", is h
or "intagl
glows mag
when lit
underne
inte

Austin
(Great Britain)

Dragonfly "Lalique"

Swift (Great Britain)

Peugeot (France)

Paige (USA)

Sunbeam
(Great Britain)

ABC (Great Britain)

Chalmers (USA)

Buick (USA)

Oldsmobile (USA)

Rover (Great Britain)

Bean (Great Britain)

Fiat (Italy)

Wolseley Siddeley
(Great Britain)

Ferrari (Italy)

Morris (Great Britain)

Hupmobile (USA)

MG (Great Britain)

Crossley (Great Britain)

Haynes (USA)

TOP MARQUE
Perhaps the most famous of all
the vanished marques, the French
Bugatti made superb, stylish cars
in the 1920s and 1930s. The
company's badge, bearing
designer Ettore Bugatti's
distinctive "EB" logo, and
the classic horseshoe
radiator, are among
the best known of all
motoring hallmarks.

Bugatti cars
and radiator

Case (USA)

s-Royce (Great
Britain)

"Spirit of Ecstasy"
mascot

E OF DISTINCTION
radiator mascots, few are
amous than Rolls-Royce's
of Ecstasy", which has
ed the bonnets of their cars
910. This statuette, along
e distinctive, temple-
radiator grille and the RR
make Rolls-Royces
ly recognizable.

Rolls-
Royce
grille

Unic (France)

Stutz (USA)

Constantinesco
(France)

CONSTANTINESCO

Index

AB

ABC, 62
aerodynamics, 32, 33, 35
Alfa Romeo, 18
Argyll, 59
Aston Martin, 19, 26
Auburn, 22, 23
Austin, 62; Mini, 30, 31;
    Seven, 24; Ten, 24, 25
"Autronic" eye, 29
axle, rear, 9, 38, 52, 53
battery, 30, 50, 51
baulk ring, gearbox, 53
Bean, 62
Bentley, 18, 19
Benz 12, 42; Velo, 6, 7
Benz, Karl, 6
big ends, engine, 45, 47
Bluebird, 58, 59
body, 16, 24, 32, 35;
    carbon-fibre, 33; fibre-
    glass, 32; styling, 22,
    23, 27, 28, 34-35; tub,
    16, 33
bonnet, 13, 17, 23, 29-30
boot, 8, 25, 26, 29
brake, 38, 56, 57; cable, 7;
    disc, 33, 38, 39, 57;
    drum, 12, 19, 24, 38,
    57; emergency
    footbrake, 9; fluid, 39;
    hydraulic, 23, 57;
    master cylinder, 57;
    pads, 57; pedal, 38;
    power-assisted, 29;
    shoes, 57; wheel
    cylinder, 57
"bubble cars", 30
Buehrig, Gordon, 23
Bugatti, 18, 19, 63
Bugatti, Ettore, 19, 63
Buick, 62

C

Cadillac, 28, 29, 30, 50
caliper, see brake, disc
Campbell, Malcolm, 58
camshaft, 42, 44, 45
carbide gas for lights, 21
carburettor, 19, 39, 48, 49
carriage lamps, 6, 20
Case, 63
Chalmers, 62
chassis, 13, 16, 26, 36
Chevrolet, 18
choke, carburettor, 48, 49
Citroen, 55
Clarion Bell, 10
clutch, 9, 38, 42, 52
coach-work, 6, 8, 12, 17,
    22
coil, 50, 51
compression, 45, 48
computers, 35, 39
Concours d'État, 23
condenser, 51
connecting rod, 42, 47
Constantinesco, 63
contact breaker, 51
cooling system, 9, 13, 39,
    42, 44
Cord, 23
crankshaft, 42, 43, 44, 45,
    46, 47
Crossley, 63
cylinder head, 46
cylinder, 42, 43, 44-45, 46,
    50

DE

Daimler, 9
damper, 38, 39, 54, 55;
    friction, 55; hydraulic,
    55; "hydrogas", 55
dashboard, 6, 27, 41
de Dion Bouton, 8-9, 10
Delage, 18
Delauney-Belville, 12
detonate, 48
differential, 53
distributor, 42, 50, 51
dogs, gearbox, 53
drag coefficient, 35
drive 52, 53; drive chain,
    6, 7, 52; leather belt, 6;
    shaft, 8, 9, 31, 38, 39
Duesenberg J, 18
Dunlop, 58, 59
Duryea brothers, 8
ear muffs, 14
Earl, Harley, 28
electrics, 12, 39, 50
engine 6-7, 9, 12-13, 17,
    18-19, 23, 25, 26-27, 29,
    30-31, 39, 42-47, 48,
    50-51, 52-53
Essex, 15
exhaust, 16, 19, 33, 38, 39,
    44-45, 46; stroke, 45

FG

fan, 39, 46
Ferrari 26, 63; 312 T4, 32,
    33; Boxer engine, 33
Fiat, 63; 500, 30; Panda,
    34; "Topolino", 30
final-drive, 7, 9, 31, 38, 53
float, carburettor, 48, 49
flywheel, 6, 42, 45, 47, 52
footwarmer, 14
Ford, 29; 1959, 28; Model
    T, 16-17, 54; V8, 45; Y,
    24
Ford, Henry, 16, 17
Formula One racing, 32
four-stroke cycle, 44, 45
front-wheel-drive, 30, 38,
    53
fuel injection, 27, 44, 48,
    49
fuel system, 17, 38; 48
fuselage, racing car, 32
gearbox, 17, 30, 31, 33, 38,
    52, 53; automatic, 53;
    manual, 53
gears, 6, 39, 52, 53;
    changing, 7, 27, 38, 52,
    53; pulleys, 6, 7
gloves and gauntlets, 14
goggles, 14
Grand Tourer, 28
grand routier, 22
Grebel, Stephen, 21
grille, 13, 25, 29, 63
ground effect, 32
GT *see Grand Tourer*, 35
gudgeon pin, 47

HI

half-shaft, 53
hand signals, 11
handbrake, 7, 9, 13, 17, 18,
    38, 56, 57
Haynes, 63
headlight 21, 23, 37, 31 41
high tension, *see ignition*
hill-climbing, 6, 52
hill-climbs, 32
Hispano-Suiza, 12
Hollywood, 22
Honda, 56
hood, "Cape-cart", 12;
    electric, 27
horn 10, 11
"horseless carriage", 6, 38
Humber, 55
Hupmobile, 63
hydraulic brake, *see brake*
ignition 7, 9, 13, 45, 50, 51
indicators, 11, 25, 45
inlet manifold, 46
Isetta, 30
Issigonis, Alec, 30

JKL

Jaguar, 2, 59
Jenkins, Ab, 23
jet, carburettor, 48, 49

MN

Lagonda, 59
Lalique, René, 62
Lauda, Niki, 33
Le Corbusier, 34
Le Mans race, 18, 19
lead (in petrol), 48
Lenoir, Étienne, 6, 48
lights, 20-21, 41, 50
Ligier, 31
limousine, 13
little end, 47
Lotus, 31
low tension, *see ignition*
Lucas lamps, 20-21

MN

magneto, 50
"Mangin" mirror, 21
maps, 15
mascot, 30, 62-63
mass-production, 16, 17,
    35, 36-37
Maserati, 26
Mercedes, 10; Mercedes-
    Benz 300 SL
    "Gullwing", 26, 27
MG, 63
Michelin, 60
Mille Miglia race, 28
Miller oil lamp, 20
Mini, see Austin Mini
Mitchell, Bill, 26
models, design, 34, 35
Morris, 59, 63
neutral, gear, 53
night driving, 20, 21
number plate, 8

OPQR

octane rating, petrol, 48
Oldsmobile 8, 62
Opel Kadett, 24
Packard, 22
Paige, 62
Panhard Levassor, 8, 12,
    23
petrol, 6, 26, 44, 45, 48, 49
Peugeot, 22, 62
Phaeton, 17
piston rings, 45, 47
piston, 42, 44, 45, 47, 50
pneumatic tyre, *see tyre*
pointless ignition, *see*
    ignition,
points, contact breaker,
    50-51
power stroke, 42-45
propeller shaft, 52
puncture, 13, 58, 60
pushrods, 47

"putties", 14
races, 500 cc, 32
racing cars, 26, 32, 33
rack, *see steering*
radiator, 17, 33, 39
rear-wheel-drive, 38, 52,
    53
Renault, 8; Four, 30; Five,
    36-41; V10, 45
rendering, 34
reverse gear, 53
rocker arms, 42, 47
Roi des Belges
    coachwork, 12
Rolls, Charles, 13
Rolls-Royce, 12, 13, 63;
    Silver Ghost, 12, 13
rotary engine, 43
rotor arm, 51
Rover, 62
Royce, Henry, 13
rpm, 42
runabout, 8, 17
running board, 17

S

saloon cars, 25
Scheckter, Jody, 33
shock absorber, *see*
    damper
sidepods, racing car, 32,
    33
silencer, 38
sill, 17, 27
Simplicorn horn, 10
skirt, racing car, 32
slicks, *see tyre*
space-frame, 26
spark plug, 19, 45, 50,
    51
speed limits, 10, 11
"Spirit of Ecstasy", 13,
    63
sports cars, 18, 23, 26, 27
springs, 54, 55; cantilever,
    54; coil, 55; leaf, 54
squab, seat, 16
starter ring, 42, 47
starting the car, 9, 50
steering, 7, 9, 38, 56-57;
    four-wheel, 56; power-
    assisted, 29; gear, 39,
    56, 57; rack and pinion,
    39, 56; wheel, 17, 38;
    worm and nut, 56, 57
straight engine, 43
stroke, piston, 45
Stutz, 62, 63
subframe, 38
sump, 43, 46
Sunbeam, 62
sunroof, 25
supercharger, 18, 23, 49

suspension, 39, 54, 55;
    independent, 55; Mi[n]
    31; pullrod, 33; racin[g]
    car, 32
Swift, 62

T

thermostat, 43
three-wheeler, 30
throttle, 7, 9, 13, 48, 49
timing belt, 43
tonneau, 19
Tourer, 17
touring, 14, 15, 22
track rod, 56
transmission, 52
trim, 19, 40-41
turbocharger, 33, 49
tyre, 60, 61; balloon, 60;
    cross-ply, 61; inner
    tube, 60, 61; low
    profile, 61; pneumati[c]
    12, 16, 54, 60-61; raci[ng]
    slicks, 32-33, 61; radi[al]
    ply, 61; solid rubber,
    56, 60; tread, 60, 61;
    tubeless, 61; whitewa[ll]
    22, 28

UVW

Unic, 63
universal joints, 52
"V" engine, 43
valve, 7, 9, 43, 44, 45, 46,[ ]
    47; springs, 43, 47;
    timing, 45
vanes, turbocharger, 49
Vauxhall, 55
venturi, carburettor, 48
Volkswagen Beetle, 30
vulcanizing, tyre, 6
Wankel engine, 43
water pump, 46
Weber carburettor, 49
wheel, 39, 58, 59; alloy,
    59; artillery, 58;
    pressed-steel disc, 5[9]
    Sankey-type, 58; spa[ke]
    38, 58, 60; wire spoke[d]
    24, 58-59; wooden
    spoked, 9, 13, 16
windscreen wipers, 13,[ ]
windscreen, 13, 14, 23,[ ]
    27, 29, 40-41
windscreen, rear, 12
wing, 16
wishbone, 39, 55
Wolseley Siddeley, 63
worm, *see steering*

Acknowledgments

**Dorling Kindersley would like
to thank:**
The National Motor Museum,
Beaulieu: pp. 6-7, 8-9, 10-11, 12-13,
14-15, 18-19, 20-21, 22-23, 24-25, 26-
27, 32-33; 58-59, 60-61, 62-63; and
especial thanks to Roger Bateman,
Tony Cooper and Derek Maidment
for their help.
The Science Museum, London: pp.
30-31, 48-49, 50-51, 54-55, 56-57.
Colin Tomlinson and Mr Parsons of
Essex Autotrim pp. 16-17, 54.
American Dream, Maidstone: pp.
28-29; and George Flight for his
valuable help.

Renault, France pp. 36-45.
Tim Jackson, Bob Gibbon, and the
staff of Renault UK for their help
with pp. 36-41.
Bryn Hughes and John Gillard of
Classic Restorations, London: pp.
46-47.
Italdesign, Turin, and the Design
Museum, London: pp. 34-35.
The Carburettor Centre, London
for the variable jet and Weber
carburettors on p. 49.
Lucas Automotive: pp. 51; with
especial thanks to Ken Rainbow.
Karl Shone for special
photography: pp. 34-35.

Peter Mann of the Science Museum
for his help with the text.
Lester Cheeseman for his desktop
publishing expertise.
Mary Ling for her research.

Picture credits

t=top b=bottom l=left r=right c=centre

Allsport 61tr
Neill Bruce: 49bl
Jean Loup Charmet: 20 bl; 23tl; 50cl;
    63bc
Colorsport :33cr; 47bl

Mary Evans Picture Library: 6bl; 8bl;
    12tr; 13tr; 16bl; 17tc; 18tl; 19tr, br; 2[ ]
    22cl; 25tr; 48cl, bl, br; 55cr; 56cr; 58t[ ]
    59bc
Ford Motor Company: 24cr
Honda UK Ltd: 56bl
Hulton Picture Library: 52cl
Jaguar Cars Ltd: 43tr
Mansell Collection: 8cl; 9cr; 14cr; 16tl[ ]
National Motor Museum: 11tr; 15tr; 2[ ]
    26cr; 38tr; 50br; 52tr
Quadrant Picture Library: 32tl
Rolls-Royce Motor Cars Ltd: 63cr
Rover Group plc: 37TC, tr; 37br

Illustration by: John Woodcock

Picture research: Cynthia Hole